MICHAEL JACKSON

The Man Behind the Mask

MICHAEL JACKSON

The Man
Behind
the Mask

An Insider's Story
of the King of Pop

An Exposé by
BOB JONES

As Told to
STACY BROWN

SelectBooks, Inc.

Michael Jackson: The Man Behind the Mask
©2009 by Bob Jones and Stacy Brown
All rights reserved.

This edition published by SelectBooks, Inc. For information address SelectBooks, Inc., New York, New York.

First paperback edition.

First hardbound edition published in 2005 by SelectBooks, Inc.

Paperback edition ISBN 978-1-59079-203-2

The Library of Congress has catalogued the original hardbound edition as follows:

Jones, Bob, 1932–
Michael Jackson, the man behind the mask : an insider's story of the king of pop / an exposé by Bob Jones as told to Stacy Brown.— 1st ed.
p. cm.
Includes bibliographical references (p.) and index.
ISBN 1-59079-072-3 (hardbound : alk. paper)
1. Jackson, Michael, 1958– 2. Rock musicians--United States--Biography.
3. Jones, Bob, 1932– 4. Public relations consultants--United States--
Biography. I. Brown, Stacy, 1968– II. Title.
ML420.J175J66 2005
782.42166'092--dc22
                        2005009020

Manufactured in the United States of America

10 9 8 7 6 5 4 3 2 1

THIS BOOK IS DEDICATED
TO THE LOVING MEMORY OF MY MOTHER
RUBY FAYE JONES,

AND ALSO TO MY FRIENDS,
THE LATE MAGGIE HATHAWAY AND BILL LANE

Contents

Prologue   *1*

Chapter 1   AN ARRESTING DEVELOPMENT   *4*

Chapter 2   FROM FORT WORTH TO HOLLYWOOD   *33*

Chapter 3   SEND ME YOUR POOR, YOUR DISENFRANCHISED *45*
              (HOWEVER, PLEASE ALLOW THEM TO BE WHITE)

Chapter 4   THE HONEYMOON   *67*

Chapter 5   THE KING AND THE PRINCESS   *83*

Chapter 6   WHAT'S LOVE GOT TO DO WITH IT?   *95*

Chapter 7   ENEMIES BE DAMNED   *101*

Chapter 8   HALL OF SHAME   *109*

Chapter 9   FINANCIAL HISTORY   *117*

Chapter 10   THE DEVIL HIMSELF   *125*

Epilogue   *135*

Afterword   THE CURRENT CASE   *141*

Acknowledgments

We are grateful beyond words for the opportunity to write the story of Bob Jones and his unique relationship with pop music's preeminent superstar, Michael Jackson.

The first bridge to this road was built by Bob Jones: The Godfather of Black Hollywood. It was his vision, honesty and memory that brought this story about.

While there were many who couldn't wait to read the words of Bob Jones, we did encounter skeptics. In the world that we live in, being skeptical is not only the politically correct way for most, but, for many, the only way.

Our agents, Bill Gladstone and Neil Gudovitz, believed in us and delivered. For this we are forever grateful. SelectBooks also believed and carried this bright torch to bookstores everywhere for us.

Among the many who contributed their time and/or assistance, we would particularly like to thank the staff at the Library of Congress and the New York City and Los Angeles Public Libraries.

Many works by other writers influenced what appears here, especially Adrian Grant's "Michael Jackson: The Visual Documentary," J. Randy Taraborrelli's *Michael Jackson: The Magic and The Madness;* Christopher Andersen's *Michael Jackson Unauthorized;* and Raymond Chandler's *All That Glitters,* and Diane Dimond for her relentless reporting on Michael Jackson for more than 10 years.

Members of the Jackson family were also helpful in sorting fact from fiction.

The dedication for this book speaks for itself, but others who advised and encouraged or otherwise should be noted include my wonderful-gift-from-God-of-a-wife, Shenay Brown (If God One Day Struck Me Blind, Your Beauty I'd Still See); my mother, Bebe McDaniel-Smith; My heart and soul Rikki Brown and Jordan Brown; Talia Smith; Devon White and family; Kaneda Brown; Justin Brown; Anthony and Carol Wyche; my bodyguard and brother Jon Dolphin; The great mayor of the marvelous city of Mount Vernon, New York Ernest D. Davis; Leslie Alpert; Phil Griffin, the VP of MSNBC Primetime Programming; George Uribe; Falguni Lakhani; Dan Abrams and his wonderful staff; the fabulous Rita Cosby; Damon Harris; Clarence and Patricia Coleman; Arlette Stewart (my favorite cousin); the Rouson Family; Spencer and Crystal Massey; Mr. and Mrs. Bobby Warren; Tisha Lewis; Dennis Love, who built the original proposal for this work and who helped make my dream of being an author a reality five years ago; and congrats to Mr. and Mrs. Jonathan Dolphin.

Prologue

B ob Jones was working through a routine day—if any day managing the public image and private affairs of troubled pop megastar Michael Jackson could possibly be considered even remotely routine—when a courier dropped a letter on his desk. The letter, generated by an attorney for Michael's brother Randy Jackson, was icily succinct: "Your services are no longer required."

And so, without a direct word between them, this frosty missive ended a 34-year relationship between Jones and Michael Jackson an association that began when the King of Pop, a moniker coined by Jones, was a 12-year-old *wünderkind* trooping through the halls of Motown Records.

Bob Jones—the immensely respected public relations guru who had guided Michael through the hailstorms and mine-fields of unprecedented celebrity for as long as anyone could remember, who had helped mold the chaotic career of the man-child who became one of the most sensational and beloved entertainers of the 20th century, who had literally and figuratively bandaged Michael back together after the self-destructive star's multiple self-inflicted wounds, who had remained superhumanly loyal amid the perpetual tumult of bizarre and illicit behavior and legal troubles and tabloid scrutiny that would have sent any other PR man to his grave long ago—was out.

Jones, the last vestige of old-school stability in a once-invincible organization that had been battered and plundered from

1

top to bottom, was shocked as much by the manner in which he was released as by the actual fact. Fired via messenger? Incredible.

The situation turned surreal when, shortly thereafter, a team arrived and began to confiscate the contents of his office. It was as if Jones had landed a cameo on an especially paranoid episode of "The X-Files."

The irony was overwhelming. Jones thought back to the 1995 Black Entertainment Television (BET) special, "Bob Jones: Godfather of Black Hollywood," produced in honor of Jones' 35th anniversary in the public relations business. During that gala, Michael had spoken movingly of Jones' loyalty. Now, loyalty be damned: Jones had himself become a victim of the same paranoia and delusion that he had witnessed Michael using against countless others, the same obsessive mistrust that Jones had long counseled Michael against. *I should have seen it coming,* he thought. Alas, he had not.

Bob Jones wasn't the only person stunned by his abrupt, unexpected and startlingly undiplomatic termination. As word spread across the entertainment world, the tributes to Jones began, as did the speculation about how to interpret this latest distress signal from the Jackson camp. Michael's team was currently trying to fend off child molestation charges in Santa Barbara County, California. Michael Jackson without Bob Jones riding shotgun? It was inconceivable.

Typical reaction came from Fox News gossip columnist Roger Friedman, who wrote: "Motown historians know the name Bob Jones. The PR whiz started working at the famed record label in 1970, where he met and represented Michael Jackson and The Jackson Five ... No matter what scandal has cropped up over the years, Jones has always been there for the self-proclaimed King of Pop. From the Elephant Man's bones to Lisa Marie to the 1993 (child molestation) settlement, Bob

Jones knows where every single body is buried in Jackoland. Imagine the possibilities."

After a summer of reflection and deliberation, Bob Jones decided to tell his story—not to any of the major media outlets here and abroad who contact him virtually every day, but in his own book. He wants to tell his story his way.

After more than four decades of service, with clients ranging from the Jackson family to Diana Ross to Bruce Willis to the late Rick James, Jones finally wanted to give a full accounting of a life and career that by sheer dint of labor and ambition landed him in the rarified circles of Hollywood. In this time, he not only learned to operate the image-making ropes and pulleys of international superstardom, but became a racial pioneer in a town and a business that had been virtually lily-white before his arrival in the 1950s.

But while Jones' own story is fascinating and instructive, as an unabashed realist he knows that in the telling his life must serve as a backdrop—albeit a powerful one—to the incredible story of his most famous client: Michael Jackson. Throughout this book, Bob's own words will be indented and set off with italics, as follows:

If I am going to write a book, I intend to give the readers what they want.

This is the first detailed, candid, and uncensored account from behind the scenes of the life and times of the world's biggest superstar: from the seminal days of The Jackson Five, to Michael's breakout solo career, to his ultimate status as one of the most dynamic and popular performers in the annals of popular music.

It was Jones who helped to chart Michael's rocket-like ascent to the top of the cutthroat music industry and into the realm of the most universally pervasive brand of celebrity imaginable, for Michael Jackson is that rare thing: a superstar. It staggered Jones the day he realized that Michael had become the most famous living person on Earth.

Jones had been along every mile of this remarkable and tragic journey, as Michael morphed from a supremely talented, ground-breaking young artist of unparalleled devotion to his craft into a hollow shell of eroding skills, immorality and isolated self-delusion. Michael's passion for music had been transformed into an obsession with his image, celebrity and diminishing fortune, and a reckless and bottomless self-indulgence.

After years of rationalizations and internal debate about what was actually happening, Jones himself was finally forced to confront some difficult truths.

> *It ate at me. Time after time. Should I quit this job? But I had to remember a couple of things: For one thing, I was assuming Michael was doing something criminal with these young boys. Even today, I have no concrete proof. Sure, I'd see these boys go into his private quarters and stay for hours, days, weeks at a time.*
>
> *The parents of these boys would also see these bizarre scenarios unfolding, but they too said nothing. I had no real evidence. Furthermore, I couldn't afford to quit and become an outcast. Jobs for black public relations men in Hollywood are extremely scarce. I envisioned quitting and being blacklisted. Not able to work. Not able to eat. No unemployment benefits.*
>
> *When I expressed my concerns over his behavior to Michael, he angrily told me to mind my business. And when I was called to testify before the Grand Jury in the 1993 child molestation case, everybody wondered what I would say. Would I tell the truth? Hell yes, I wasn't going to jail for anyone, not even Michael Jackson.*

After years of dodged prosecutions, tens of millions in secret hush-money payouts to parents of "little friends" and one very public settlement with the family of the "Rent-a-

Wreck Family" case, Jones is now prepared to discuss Michael's behavior with these boys—some of them child stars and household names.

Michael had a sinister gift for identifying these boys; it was as if he had some sort of radar. I was continually amazed by how he could determine which of the many children he came into contact with might be "woo-able," whose parents could be bought off and counted on to keep quiet about what was going on. I came to understand that Michael manipulated people and events with a great deal of finesse.

There was one kid, Louie Paulsen, with whom Michael managed to carry on a clandestine relationship for years. (Louie Paulsen is a pseudonym, as will be the other names I give Michael's young friends throughout this book.) Louie and his parents traveled with us around the world throughout 1988 and 1989 on the "Bad" tour. Michael and Louie spent virtually all their time together.

Timmy slept in Michael's room at night. In the afternoons, schedule permitting, in whatever exotic foreign city we were in, Michael would make chauffeur-driven cars available to Louie's parents for shopping sprees, entertainment, sight seeing and other diversions, clearing the way for hours alone together with Louie in the privacy of his hotel room.

In Paris I told Michael, "The press is going to start asking questions about all these little white boys you keep around." When I said that he grew irritated and replied, "Who cares what they think?"

Back in those days, Michael did take some pains to obscure the presence of his young companions. In 1992 we traveled to Africa, primarily to the Republic of Gabon, in what was billed as a goodwill tour.

The truth was that the government of Gabon paid for Michael's visit. Michael didn't "do" goodwill tours; he always insisted on being paid, whether it was over or under the table. The King of Pop insisted that his every public appearance was to be a major event, so the media was teeming around us like ants on the morning we were to depart LAX for Africa.

Michael's limo arrived at the airport, stopping first before it reached the media area. One of Jackson's security guards signaled me to come over to the car. I looked inside and there was yet another of Michael's little friends: Sitting next to Michael was Damon Patrick, a very cute boy.

During this African trip, this boy's parents stayed home in Australia. Don't ask me how Michael managed to convince them to allow their child to travel halfway around the globe without them, but, clearly part of my job was to keep the kid out of the spotlight. We tucked him into a seat among the luggage. Michael got out of the car to great attention. Then the chauffeur drove the car to the other side of the plane, unloading the boy out of view of the cameras.

We flew to Gabon and then to Tanzania, Kenya and Morocco. That trip was notable because a high-ranking U.S. State Department official traveled with us, primarily to run interference and grease the skids as we traveled from country to country.

All of us, including the State Department official, and Jet Magazine Publisher Bob Johnson, saw the boy enter Michael's private bedroom numerous times and remain for a long time. Characteristically, Michael did whatever he wanted to do—hang the risk.

The Australian Damon grew up to be a handsome young man, maintaining a friendship with Michael even after they stopped sleeping together. This was unusual: Michael normally lost all interest in his young friends once the boys reached the age of 13.

Michael's reckless behavior was increasingly worrisome. During a trip to Monte Carlo with a young Rent-a-Wreck Family member (as he became known amongst us, for reasons you will later understand), I told Michael's secretary, Norma Staikos, "This boy is going to cost a lot of money." Eventually, Michael was *accused of molesting the little boy. It cost the King of Pop tens of millions to settle with the boy and his family.*

Secretary Norma Staikos was a piece of work in her own right. During the Rent-a-Wreck Family investigation, the authorities concluded that it was she who arranged travel for Michael and many of his special guests, and it looked like they might turn the screws on her in order to prosecute Michael.

But then one day she was gone: she moved to Greece, out of the authorities' reach, to Michael's considerable benefit. Still, Norma stayed in touch. Every so often, she would leave a message for Michael at MJJ Productions and with his assistant: "I need $70,000," or "I need $100,000."

Whatever amount requested, it was always sent without question or delay. She's probably been paid millions. And people wonder what happened to all of Michael's money. In fact, Michael's former business manager, Myung Ho Lee, testified in his lawsuit against Michael that whenever Norma called for money, it was sent to her. Lee, who settled his suit against Michael Jackson in 2002, said Norma was always given money upon request. He speculated that it was to keep her quiet.

Those of us in Michael's inner circle also grew to understand just how out of touch Michael was with other celebrities. For example, when Michael was introduced to Michael Jordan on the set of the "Jam" video, one of his little friends had to explain to him who the NBA superstar was. Michael had never heard of him. Michael Jordan was probably at the apex of his own celebrity then, at that point the only person whose fame rivaled Michael Jackson's ... and the King was oblivious.

Perhaps the most outrageous examples of Michael's determination to obscure the truth about his sexual proclivities were his two marriages, the most notorious of which was his short-lived union with Lisa Marie Presley.

These inauthentic marriages were public relations nightmares, most notably with Lisa Marie. The poor girl seemed genuinely smitten with Michael before she realized that she had been the victim of a heartless scam.

Michael had pursued Lisa Marie for the supposed boost of testosterone it provided his image—not to mention his desire to gain control of the Elvis Presley songbook (much as he had gained copyrights to The Beatles' work) and the rest of the massive Presley estate.

According to Jones, Michael's life is full of these self-serving manipulations. Obsessed with being viewed as royalty (hence his insistence on being referred to as "The King of Pop"), Michael ardently campaigned for British knighthood. His efforts were, however, ignored by the Queen.

Undeterred, Michael flagrantly depicted himself as a close friend of Princess Diana, even appearing with Barbara Walters after Diana's death to discuss their friendship. In actuality, they had met only once, and Diana had immediately identified Michael as an opportunist. Princess Diana then joined a lengthy list of famous people who refused to take Michael's calls. Even Oprah Winfrey failed to return calls for the King's manager, Sandy Gallin.

The list of Michael's deviancies, manipulations, and schemes gets longer and longer. Behind every benevolent gesture, it seems, lay an ulterior motive. The legendary Neverland Ranch, replete with its zoo animals and carnival rides, is presented as a magical panorama for children, created by a man isolated by fame and cheated out of his own childhood. In reality, it is viewed by Jackson insiders like Jones as an enormously expensive lure, the ultimate candy from a stranger.

Another example: Michael was the single largest financial contributor to the Million Man March, but his concern wasn't African-American empowerment. His actual aim was to buy favor from Nation of Islam leader Louis Farrakhan. Michael wanted Farrakhan to apply pressure on a consortium of high-profile Hollywood players who were then cold-shouldering Michael in the wake of his controversial (some claimed anti-Semitic) song, "They Don't Care About Us." Farrakhan ultimately refused to intervene in the matter, infuriating Michael.

This cunning Michael became the predominant personality with whom Bob Jones was forced to deal in the latter stages of their association. Gone was the naïve, gentle, bright-spirited young man who had once captivated Jones and the world at large. Instead, here was a man of nearly unrelenting cynicism and dark intentions, a man who despised the praise über-producer Quincy Jones received for his work on Michael's "Thriller" and "Bad" albums, work that represented the pinnacle of Michael's career. The cunning Michael shunned his parents and siblings. He thought so little of himself and his heritage that he resorted to ruinous plastic surgery to alter his looks, taking injections to whiten his skin (despite his many denials about this).

Michael's judgment grew more impaired by the day, demonstrated by his increasingly careless behavior with omnipresent young boys, and misguided decisions such as bringing in the Nation of Islam to manage his affairs.

The 2003 charges of child molestation brought in Santa Barbara raised the stress and turmoil to an unprecedented level. By the time Jones was fired, the Jackson Empire had been brought so low that Jones had been forced to move his operations as vice president of MJJ Productions to his home office in L.A.

Jones and the rest of MJJ had once occupied some of the most prime commercial real estate on Los Angeles' pristine Sunset Strip, but that lease had been lost, and the company could no longer afford office space.

When Jones' firing came, it was a shock and an insult, yes, but it was also something of a relief. Because of their many years together, his commitment to the Jackson family, and because Jones believed Michael's essential goodness still existed somewhere deep inside, Jones never would have deserted Michael in this hour of need.

But if Michael believed he didn't need Bob Jones—well, so be it. The cherry on top came when one of the Jackson attorneys told Jones there would be no severance pay, no retirement package. "You know there's no money," the lawyer told him. "It should have been enough of an honor just to work with Michael Jackson." It was over.

1

An Arresting Development

*"An arrest warrant for Mr. Jackson has been issued
on multiple counts of child molestation ..."*

—Santa Barbara County Sheriff Jim Anderson,
November 19, 2003

As sheriff and officials from the District Attorney's office gathered at a news conference some 393 miles away in Los Olivos, California, Michael Jackson sat in a Las Vegas hotel suite, denying to his family this latest round of child sex abuse allegations. Hurrying to Michael's side upon learning of the latest episode in the fallen King of Pop's life, it was obvious to all that this latest disaster all but put to bed any hopes of Michael returning to the top of the music charts.

With the pressure, embarrassment, and fury that came with the disgraceful charges, Michael remained Michael: cocky, undaunted, and ice cold toward family members who publicly bent over backwards to demonstrate their love.

One moment captured the essence of the man in the mirror, or the man behind the surgically-meshed-together face. It was when Michael's equally famous sister Janet arrived at the Las Vegas hotel to offer her brother moral support and sisterly affection.

Michael had these choice words for his lil' sister: "You still won't break any of my records, *Diva!* You will never outsell me!"

11

A broken-hearted Janet unsuccessfully tried to compose herself as she exited the room in tears. Janet had to be comforted by her older sister Rebbie (widely known as the only "normal" Jackson).

This is the Michael Jackson Bob Jones had come to know after nearly twenty years heading MJJ Productions, and running constant interference for Michael with the relentless media looking to cop any story about the erstwhile King of Pop.

Michael made it perfectly clear that he didn't want his family around. It didn't matter what was currently going on. He ordered his staff to stay away from them and to keep them at arm's length from him. Janet was a problem in that she was the one Jackson who managed to escape Michael's financial manipulations.

Unlike the rest of the family, Michael couldn't control Janet. He failed to recognize that she was able to become almost *as* big, if not *as* big, as he in the world of popular music.

He signed the rest of the family, including the nieces and nephews, to his label and refused to let any of their music get out. Signing family members to his MJJ record label—a label presented him after he signed a reported $1 billion deal with Sony Music in 1988—was one of the many tools Michael used to ensure that he would be the only Jackson with music on the airwaves. By signing them to long-term contracts and promising them that their recordings would be released and promoted, Michael had the entire family at his beck and call.

Of course he'd duck their repeated phone calls and inquiries about their music, and he would rarely allow them to cut an album. There were notable exception; Michael had a special affinity for the group 3T.

Taj, Tarryl and Tito Jackson Jr. (sons of Tito Jackson), found incredible success in the UK after Michael finally fulfilled a contractual obligation by releasing their album overseas. Those kids were seen as heartthrobs to Europeans across the continent. Their record was a smash until, you guessed it, Michael became aware of it. He then hurried to stop it, rushing the boys back to the United States with promises of stateside grandeur.

The other exception of Michael fulfilling, or at least pretending to fulfill, his contractual obligation, was to his older sister Rebbie. After five years working on her 1997 album, "Yours Faithfully," the title track was released. Rebbie was in the spotlight for the first time since her 1995 debut "Centipede." One month into the "Yours Faithfully" campaign, Michael ordered the record pulled. It was too much success and notoriety for a sibling. He couldn't stomach it.

Michael often inquired about what Rebbie and Jermaine were trying to do musically, as well as outside of music. Former Los Angeles Police Detective Bill Bray became Michael's security chief and confidante and was often the point man Michael used to gather information on people, including Michael's own family.

When not digging up dirt on them, he was scheming to prevent them from performing. One of Michael's favorite methods was to make promises to A & R people, DJs, record executives, and others. He'd either pay them off not to work with his family or he'd use his influence—dangling carrots, if you will—to executives, promising either to attend an important function, perform for them, or do something else to appease them. Most times these people would kowtow to Michael and, following his wishes, shun his family.

Janet was the exception. Michael didn't have a clue as to what little sis was doing. He thought she was interested in pursuing an acting career. He was both stunned and dismayed when she "slipped through the cracks" and became a musical force all her own.

Janet's career was spearheaded by John McClain, who later came to work for Michael. To get the job with Michael, McClain had to agree that he'd never again work with Janet Jackson (though I was told Janet had a falling out with John McClain, so there was no real need for him to try and return to Janet's employ). The rule was simple: Once you work with the King of Pop, you can never work with another Jackson family member.

Because Michael was unable to control Janet, he seemed to endorse her separation from the Jackson family.

It was bought to my attention by his assistant that the King had a letter drafted to Janet letting her know that she could legally divorce herself from the family. Although there are no restrictions upon her use of her own actual last name, Michael hated the fact that another Jackson was upstaging him. He was trying to manipulate his sister into just being called Janet. Then of course, ridiculously enough, Michael could have then still laid claim to be the only superstar Jackson. This letter was never forwarded to Janet, but what is interesting is that for a short time she did publicly become simply Janet—not Janet Jackson.

Janet had first come into the consciousness of the American public at the age of seven when she appeared with brother Randy on the Jackson family's CBS television special. Playing straight man to his baby sister's adorably sassy Mae West imitation, Randy obviously caught on that Janet was the star.

By age nine Janet had penned her first tune, perhaps inspired by the Jackson Five's success. But father Joseph Jackson had a different plan for Janet. Although the Jackson Five had proven themselves a commercial success in music, in Joseph's opinion acting would provide considerably more security for Janet.

Consequently, while still a child, Janet auditioned for and earned the role of Penny on the 1970s sitcom "Good Times," a spin-off of the Bea Arthur show "Maude" (which was itself a spin-off of the popular Carol O'Connor sitcom, "All in the Family").

Janet later appeared as Charlene on the hit series "Diff'rent Strokes" and Cleo on "Fame." Eventually, and unbeknownst to

Michael Jackson, Janet left "Fame" to begin her recording career with A & M Records.

Her album "Control" exploded onto the music scene in 1986. Its title track was a personal anthem to which teenagers across the world could relate. Throughout the album, producers Jimmy Jam and Terry Lewis' distinguished beats meshed gracefully with Janet's vocals. Janet used the album to reach fans and to establish an identity for herself separate from her famous family.

In 1987 Janet released "Rhythm Nation 1814." The album introduced the world to a hard-hitting Janet clad in military attire, backed by a veritable army of dancers whose aim it was to spread a message of love that was neither naïve nor superficial.

Michael Jackson had previously shown a similar propensity for military-style videos and, mimicking Janet, his public outcries for love and peace grew louder.

Janet's "Rhythm Nation 1814" led to the signing of the largest contract in music history. The thirty-million-dollar contract committed Janet to three albums with Virgin records—a label whose name stood in playful contrast to the image that Janet was now beginning to reveal.

Janet had begun to upstage Michael.

As a unit, and mostly without Michael, the rest of the family recorded the album "2300 Jackson Street" in 1989. Michael appeared in the video for the song and then, as usual, used his unmitigated influence to have the album pulled out of circulation. Its success could have provided the family with wealth independent of Michael, and the King wouldn't let that happen.

Truth be told: Michael Jackson had more than an active dislike for the Jacksons; he acted as if he despised his family.

The Jackson Five began the 1970s with the release of their first single on Motown Records "I Want You Back." The single shot to the top of the music charts. Soon the Jackson Five were famous. A series of hits followed "I Want You Back," including "ABC," "The Love You Save," and "I'll Be There."

By 1973, however, a frenetic release schedule had worn out the group's welcome. They were no longer a fixture at the top of the music charts and their songs were no longer blockbusters.

The brother's late 1973 album "Get It Together" suggested a possible new direction for the group. Its title song became a favorite in underground dance clubs. The album closed with "Dancing Machine," a track that generated interest. When it was retooled on the "Dancing Machine" album the following year, the song became one of the first true disco smash hits. "Dancing Machine" put the brothers on the top of the R & B music chart and in the Pop top ten for the first time in three years. The Jackson brothers became a fixture on dance club play lists for the next decade. The "Dancing Machine" album was followed by "Moving Violation."

> It was around this time that I remember Joseph Jackson managing a band called MDLT Willis. It was a girl-group and it seemed that Joseph and the Jackson boys were hell-bent on getting Michael to lose his virginity.
>
> So it was arranged for one of the girls in the group to go into Michael's hotel room and seduce him. But Michael had no interest in the girl or, it seems, sex. The girl was so angry that she pushed him out on the balcony, according to Rose Fine, who tutored Michael at the time. She had to stop the current concert tour because of this.. Michael was frazzled and everyone else seemed puzzled.

The Jackson Five later dropped the track "Forever Came Today" and it became a 1975 disco hit. Frustrated by creative barriers put up by Motown's management, the Jackson Five elected to leave Motown in 1976. After a fierce legal battle, Motown won the right to keep the Jackson Five name so the group adopted the name "The Jacksons."

Jermaine Jackson—now the son-in-law of Motown founder Berry Gordy—remained with Motown as a solo artist, and Randy replaced him in the group. Epic became the Jackson's new home, and they were immediately put to work with Kenny Gamble and Leon Huff, the writing and producing team behind the origins of the Philadelphia Sound.

While the Jacksons' next album featured the pop hit "Enjoy Yourself," unfortunately, sales of 1977's "Goin' Places" proved yet another disappointment.

After that, the Jacksons were finally allowed to produce and write their own material for the 1978 "Destiny" album. The result was one of their best recordings. The album featured the platinum-selling "Shake Your Body" single and a more mature Michael Jackson. The brothers went on a successful world tour.

Meanwhile, Michael emerged as an adult star of his own with his 1979 "Off The Wall" album, produced by Quincy Jones. "Triumph," the 1980 album by the Jacksons, proved likeable, with such hits as "Can You Feel It," "Lovely One" and "Walk Right Now."

After another successful group tour, Michael Jackson continued his ascent as a solo megastar with the release of "Thriller" in December 1982.

The next group album did not appear until 1984. "Victory" included a reunion with Jermaine, becoming the first album officially recorded by all six Jackson brothers. Its leadoff single "State of Shock," with rock guitar and a guest appearance by Mick Jagger, scored big on the music charts.

The union of all six Jackson brothers was short-lived, however. When the final Jacksons' studio album "2300 Jackson Street" was released in 1989, it included just Jackie, Tito, Jermaine and Randy. Michael provided a cameo on the title track and shortly thereafter maneuvered backstage that the album would not sell, which led to its being pulled from the shelves.

Michael's feelings toward his family weren't lost on his brother Jermaine, who had given Michael a dose of reality medication. Jermaine—who the world knows has been more recently been shilling for Michael on television at any mere mention of scandal—back in 1991 recorded a song called "Word to the Badd." The lyrics told the story of familial deceit on Michael's part and should have lain to rest the so-called rumors about all the plastic surgeries and the reasons behind them. Long before Michael told Oprah Winfrey and 100 million television viewers around the world that he had a rare skin disease called vitiligo, which whitened his skin, Jermaine dropped dime.

On "Word to the Badd," Jermaine sang:

"Reconstructed, been abducted, don't know who you are. Think they love you, they don't know you, lonely superstar ... .Once you were made, you changed your shade; was your color wrong? Could not turn back, it's a known fact, you were too far gone ... "

Was Michael pissed? Is his middle name Joseph?

Michael furiously phoned his mother and told her to order Jermaine out of Hayvenhurst, the Encino, California compound where Jermaine, Jermaine's wife and children and the Jackson parents still live today.

You see, Michael owns the compound and pays its bills. Katherine, the family's matriarch, pleaded with Michael. Jermaine had nowhere else to go. By this time, Jermaine and Hazel Gordy had long divorced and Jermaine no longer had the financial backing of Berry Gordy and Motown. Katherine insisted that Michael and Jermaine talk and make up. But Jermaine learned, once and for all, that if you cross Michael Jackson, publicly embarrassing him in any way, you are history.

Katherine finally persuaded Michael to let Jermaine stay at the Hayvenhurst estate, but on the rare occasions that Michael would visit the mansion, Jermaine had to make himself scarce.

Ironically, Jermaine's song was released the same week as Michael's 1991 hit single "Black or White." The two Jackson brothers war went public. Tabloid reports of dysfunction in the family increased, as did Michael's disdain for Jermaine.

According to Jermaine Jackson, producers L.A. Reid and Babyface duped him into making the song. The producers have steadfastly refused to comment on the song and when Stacy Brown met Babyface on a flight from New York to Los Angeles in 2004, Babyface refused to comment on Jermaine's story and shrugged it off.

Jermaine Jackson told co-author of this book, Stacy Brown, that he was "in Atlanta recording my album with L.A. Reid and Babyface as producers. Next thing I knew they were on a plane to California because Michael had called and said he wanted to work with them. I called Michael and we got into it. But, as it turned out, when L.A. and Babyface got with Michael, he wouldn't let them behind the boards. They found that he just wanted to control them that he really had no real interest in working with them. They came back and they did this song. They promised it wouldn't be released. They lied."

Ana after the song's release, of course, hell broke out at Hayvenhurst. To this day, Michael and Jermaine maintain a frosty relationship at best. Jack Gordon, the former husband of sister LaToya Jackson, told Fox Television that Jermaine was a "jealous animal, jealous of anyone with success in the family."

In-law Gordon insisted that LaToya told him that when Michael's "Thriller" album was released, Jermaine made comments that Michael wanted to be white and that he would not be successful. The jealousy Gordon referred to had earlier reared its head during the Jackson's 1984 "Victory" Tour. During an interview at that time Jermaine Jackson said that even though Michael Jackson "is very talented, a lot of his success has been due to timing and a little bit of luck. It could have been him, or it could just as easily have been me. But now I'm doing a lot of things. I'm the hottest brother. It'll be the same when my brothers do their thing."

Journalist Michael Roberts who creatively handed out *faux* awards to the Jackson clan famously and brilliantly captured the dysfunction in the family in a March 1994 story. Wrote Roberts at Westword.com:

> In February NBC aired a show dubbed "The Jackson Family Honors," whose real purpose was to demonstrate that the Jackson family-parents Joseph and Katherine and kids Janet, Michael, Rebbie, Tito, Randy, Jackie, Marlon and Jermaine-weren't really as dysfunctional as they seemed.
>
> Instead, this excruciating program proved that the Jacksons themselves should have won a trophy-for nerve.
>
> They deserve plenty of other plaudits, too, as the following Jackson Family "dishonors"—drawn from La Toya Jackson's ghostwritten autobiography La Toya—prove.
>
> Just in time for the April 24 McNichols Arena appearance by Janet Jackson (the only member of the family who still has a viable career); we give credit where credit is due.
>
> **BEST COSTUMES** Joseph, who enjoyed putting on grotesque latex monster masks and going outside the family home to tap on his children's bedroom windows in the dead of night. When the children went to investigate the noises, he would scream at them.
>
> **MOST SUPPORTIVE SPOUSE** Katherine, who responded to complaints from her children about their father's psychotic behavior by leaning back in her chair, laughing, and saying, "That Joseph, he's so crazy."
>
> **MOST SUPPORTIVE SIBLING** Janet, who responded to Jermaine's request that she serve as the opening act for his late-Eighties comeback tour by sneering, "He hasn't had a hit in years, and he wants me to open for him?"

MOST SUPPORTIVE UNCLE Michael, who saved his nieces' and nephews' first soiled diapers as mementoes.

MOST SUPPORTIVE PARENT Katherine, who told Marlon that he was a terrible dancer and later responded to questions about her opinion of his first solo album, Baby Tonight, with the comment, "Marlon can't sing. Why doesn't he just hang it up? He has no talent."

MOST AROMATIC JACKSON Michael, nicknamed "Smelly" by Quincy Jones because, during the recording of the Off the Wall album, he refused to shower or change his clothes for days at a time.

BRAVEST JACKSON Rebbie, who, responding to news that Michael had received a death threat before a family show, refused to go on stage, saying, "Don't you realize I can get shot? What if they decide to get him while I'm right next to him?"

BEST TABLE MANNERS Jermaine, who would "breathe" on other people's desserts before they could eat them.

BEST SCAPEGOAT Jackie, who was blamed for anything that went wrong. Joseph frequently slapped him in public.

BEST PHRASEMAKER Janet, who referred to Brooke Shields as "Giraffe Butt."

SECOND-BEST PHRASEMAKER La Toya, who referred to having sex with a man as "liking him."

BEST SIBLING RELATIONSHIP Michael and La Toya, who wanted to star together as lovers in one of Michael's videos.

BEST HUMANITARIAN Katherine, who said, "There's one mistake Hitler made in his life—he didn't kill all those Jews."

BEST ACTOR Joseph, who liked to burst unannounced into his children's rooms and scream, "I am the Jo Jo! I am the hawk!"

BEST ACTRESS Janet, who, while performing with her family in Las Vegas, portrayed Jeanette MacDonald and Cher.

BEST LOSER Michael, who, when he didn't sweep the 1980 Grammy Awards, burst into tears and cried, "How can they do this? This is so wrong!"

BEST TASTE IN MEN La Toya, who referred to George Michael as "so cute!" and Julio Iglesias as "so handsome."

MOST OLD-FASHIONED JACKSON La Toya, who was told by Iglesias after a kiss, "La Toya, you kiss like a grandmother!"

BEST TASTE IN MUSIC Katherine, whose favorite musical performer was Floyd Cramer, best known for his 1961 version of "San Antonio Rose."

BEST FAMILY MEN Joseph and Jermaine, who each fathered children with women other than their wives while they were still married.

QUICKEST-THINKING JACKSON Rebbie, who was able to stop her father from beating her mother by hitting him over the head with a shoe.

MOST UNDERRATED SEX SYMBOL Tito, whose career-endangering marriage shadowy, unnamed record company executives tried to prevent by threatening to push or drive his beloved off a cliff.

BEST-BUILT JACKSON Janet, who Michael declared had the fattest thighs in the family.

MOST BORING JACKSON Randy, about whom even La Toya can't come up with much to say.

BEST RELATIONSHIP WITH THE PRESS La Toya, who says she was glad she posed nude in *Playboy* because it forever squelched the rumor that she and Michael were the same person.

SECOND-BEST RELATIONSHIP WITH THE PRESS Michael, who stopped granting interviews after a journalist quoted him as saying he enjoyed watching children starve to death.

BEST NEWS FOR THOSE HOPING JANET JACKSON'S CONCERT WILL GO OFF WITHOUT A HITCH The rest of her family isn't planning to attend.

Court TV's Diane Dimond—known for her investigative and award-winning reporting on the Jackson family, including breaking news about the current case—further laid bare one of the family's darkest secrets when she exposed the strange familial relationships among Jermaine, Randy and Randy's wife Alejandra Jackson.

Randy Jackson had broken up with Alejandra after the couple had three children together. Alejandra then became smitten with Jermaine and they later had two children of their own.

Randy's three children currently live with Jermaine and Alejandra and their children at the Jackson family's Encino compound, Hayvenhurst. Said Dimond on Court TV's "Catherine Crier Live": "Do the children call Jermaine Uncle or Daddy or what?

> *Believe it or not, many people with whom I've spoken have said Katherine Jackson is the real source of all that ails that Jackson family. LaToya claimed in her book that her mother was an enabler to Michael's evil deeds, a silent collaborator. And Joseph, incredibly, sold stories to the tabloids about Michael and his family whenever he needed money.*

> *During all the years I worked for Michael we rarely had quiet moments. Still, despite the chaos, I enjoyed the ride. Who wouldn't have? Think about this. Early on working for Michael, we went to Rome where he played the Coliseum. Michael performed for three nights, with 55,000 people at each show. I had never seen anything like it. It was out of this world to see that one black man had drawn all these people. We went to Paris and the audiences kept growing. Ditto London, where Michael played five nights at the famed Wembley Football Stadium; 72,000 people came out each night to see him perform. All for one black man.*

Before its demise, Wembley Stadium had become the center for big crowd entertainment from rugby to rock, boxing to opera—and of course the country's national sport, soccer. All the biggest rock groups of the sixties and seventies performed at Wembley: the Rolling Stones, Pink Floyd, The Eagles, Genesis. Each is inscribed in its Hall of Fame. And the legend continued. In 1990 Madonna attracted 220,000 people, only to be outdone by Michael Jackson, who crammed the stadium for a five-concert sell out in 1992 with 370,000 fans.

I saw white folks passing out and fainting and this sort of stuff, and I couldn't believe it. Take the president and mayors and our governors and put them all in a stadium together and you couldn't draw 20,000 people, but to see Michael, this black man, draw 72,000; it was thrilling.

Still, I thought Michael too would sometime yearn for some quiet. That he too, at times, would want some down time. Wrong. Michael never wants to be ignored. For example, after the firestorm caused by his dangling of his baby son out of a Berlin hotel window, British journalist Martin Bashir still retained his all-access pass into Michael's private universe.

Michael Jackson let Martin Bashir film everything, including the children (albeit with masks covering their faces), Neverland and many shopping and vacation trips. More importantly (especially, as it turned out, to investigators in Santa Barbara), Michael allowed Bashir to film him hugging and holding hands with a young boy while pronouncing that there was nothing wrong with having little kids sleep in his bed with him.

Many news organizations in Great Britain panned the Martin Bashir documentary. Most stories led by saying that Michael Jackson admitted in a television documentary that he loves to have young boys sleep in his bed. They quoted Jackson as saying everyone should share their beds with young children. "It's what the whole world should do," one *London Times* account quoted Jackson telling interviewer Martin Bashir. The *Times* summarized:

> Both Jackson and the cancer patient claim no sexual contact occurred during the sleepovers at Jackson's Neverland ranch in California.
>
> Ten years ago, parents of thirteen-year-old [Rent-a-Wreck Family] accused Jackson of sexually molesting their son during overnight stays at his 3,000-acre ranch.
>
> After reaching a multimillion-dollar settlement with Jackson, the family dropped the case and no charges were brought against the pop star.
>
> Nevertheless, Tom Sneddon, the district attorney in charge of the [Rent-a-Wreck Family] investigation, will be paying close attention to the new allegations of Jackson "sleeping with boys" when the program airs in the U.S. Friday.
>
> According to many reports, Jackson granted the interview to Bashir, best known for interviewing Princess Diana, to help rehabilitate his troubled reputation.

According to a *London Telegraph* account the singer, when questioned by Bashir about the settlement with Rent-a-Wreck Family, said, "I didn't want to do a long drawn-out thing [trial] on TV like O.J. [Simpson] and all that stupid stuff. It wouldn't look right. I said, 'Look, let's get this over with. I want to go on with my life. This is ridiculous. I've had enough.'"

> Bashir assumed that since the [Rent-a-Wreck Family] scandal, Jackson was now more circumspect about his houseguests.
>
> But to his "utter astonishment" the interviewer said he discovered while visiting Jackson on his Neverland ranch that children were still sleeping over, "sometimes in his house, sometimes in his bedroom."
>
> One 12-year-old boy told Bashir that he slept in the singer's bed. Commenting on that occasion, Jackson said he had slept on the

floor that night, feeling he was "four" not 44, reported the Telegraph. "I see God in the face of children," said Jackson. "And man, I just love being around them all the time."

Although he claimed only "very few" boys had actually stayed in his bed, Jackson strongly defended the practice, saying: "Why can't you share your bed? The most loving thing to do is to share your bed with someone."

Despite persistent questioning from Bashir, Jackson defended his desire to sleep close to young boys, describing the practice as "very charming" and "very sweet."

In fact, he recommended that the interviewer do likewise, sleeping in the same bed with his own children as friends do.

According to Jackson, not only do children like to be touched, but the superstar told Bashir he would kill himself if he could not be close to young boys.

The 12-year-old cancer patient said he met Jackson two years ago, and began sleeping overnight at the superstar's Neverland ranch with his brother and sister.

The boy was heard on the documentary saying, "I was like, 'Michael, you can sleep in the bed,' and he was like 'No, no, you sleep on the bed,' and I was like 'No, no, no, you sleep on the bed' and then he said 'Look if you love me you'll sleep in the bed.' I was like, 'Oh man.' So I finally slept on the bed. But it was fun that night."

"We have guest units," Jackson told the interviewer, "but whenever kids come here they always want to stay with me. They say: 'Can I stay with you tonight?' So I go, 'If it's okay with your parents, then yes you can.'"

Michael Jackson told Bashir that "I tuck them in and put a little like, er, music on and when it's story time I read a book and we go to sleep with the fireplace on. I give them hot milk, you know. We have cookies. It's very charming. It's very sweet. It's what the whole world should do.

"If there were no children on this earth, if someone announced all kids were dead, I would jump off the balcony immediately."

The Bashir interview helped to show the entire world what many in Michael's inner circle had seen for years. And soon after, there was Michael in handcuffs, being led into the Santa Barbara police station like a common criminal. Dignity be damned: Michael had lost it all now for sure. The media would be relentless, which was a job that usually fell into Bob Jones' lap. But not this time.

On April 21, 2004 a grand jury indicted Michael Jackson on ten felony counts:

4 counts of lewd acts involving a minor under the age of 14

4 counts of administering an intoxicant agent (wine)

1 count of attempting a lewd act upon a minor

1 conspiracy count, which includes child abduction, false imprisonment and extortion.

Michael Jackson was arraigned April 30, 2004, and pleaded not guilty to all charges. His accuser is a young teenager whose name has not been publicly revealed (although many media outlets have discovered and published it). The boy claims the molestation took place in February and March of 2003 at Neverland Ranch.

At this point, none of this can really be called "evidence." The whole case is still "he said/he said," and might in fact remain that way through the eventual trial.

Astonishingly Michael Jackson admittedly made a $2 million payoff to the son of a Neverland maid, Blanca Francia, also in response to accusations of molestation.

Shortly after hearing pretrial testimony from the mother of Michael Jackson's accuser, Michael's attorney told reporters at a press conference in September 2004 outside the Santa Maria courthouse that Michael Jackson "would never harm a child" and he now regrets his past out-of-court settlements years ago with two children who had accused him of wrongdoing.

Attorney Thomas Mesereau Jr. said all sorts of Jackson accusers have constantly made "efforts to exploit, undermine, and take advantage of this wonderful human being. As a result, many years ago, he did pay money rather than litigate two false allegations that he harmed children. People who intended to earn millions of dollars from his record and music promotions did not want negative publicity from these lawsuits interfering with their profits," Mesereau said, with Jackson at his side. "Michael Jackson now regrets making these payments. ... These settlements were entered into with one primary condition-that condition was that Mr. Jackson never admitted any wrongdoing. Mr. Jackson always denied doing anything wrong. Mr. Jackson had hoped to buy peace in the process."

Mesereau went on to say that Jackson has made more than $1 billion in his career and, taken in that light, the settlements "were actually very small compared to money he could make in music. Mr. Jackson now realizes the advice he received was wrong. He should have fought these actions to the bitter end and vindicated himself."

Michael Jackson, dressed in a white suit and sporting black sunglasses, walked with his entourage to nearby SUVs, stopping to wave at hundreds of supporters who cheered behind a chain-link fence. He then left.

In February 2003, when the current boy accuser and his mother told child welfare officials that Michael Jackson had never acted improperly toward him, a member of Jackson's staff was present, which could have been an intimidating factor.

Court records and testimony show that the boy's mother claims Jackson gave him wine and sleeping pills, and then kept him, her, and the boy's brother as "virtual prisoners" at Neverland.

Jackson wrote "love letters" and poems to the boy, in which he called him "Rubba"—apparently a reference to a game they played together. While this is not explicit evidence of molestation, would you want to be Jackson's lawyer explaining this nickname to a jury?

The younger brother of the boy accusing Jackson reportedly witnessed "at least one act of molestation" and is said to be providing information to investigators.

Retired Santa Barbara County Sheriff Jim Thomas told an NBC audience that there was a second boy who claimed to have been molested in 1993; in fact the second boy has now testified in the trial that Michael Jackson did molest him. Unlike the boy whose family accepted a multi-million dollar settlement and then refused to cooperate in a criminal case against Jackson, this boy and his family never pressed charges.

Both Michael Jackson's fingerprints and those of his accuser were reportedly found on a pornographic magazine at Michael Jackson's ranch. Sheriff's investigators later testified to this in court during the prosecution case against Michael Jackson.

The Bashir documentary, "Living with Michael Jackson" may have led to this conflict between Jackson and the boy's family. So-called "Jackson sources" say the boy's mother demanded financial compensation for her son's on-film appearance. (The producers had neglected to have the mother sign a waiver.) When Michael Jackson refused to pay up, he and the boy's family became estranged.

According to Michael's now former attorney Mark Geragos, dozens of other visitors to Neverland will testify that they never saw the accusing boy or any other child being molested, that Jackson was rarely if ever alone with the boy.

Also problematic is that the boy's father questions the charges, saying his former wife might be encouraging his son to make false accusations. During the boy's parents' divorce proceedings, his father was accused of spousal abuse and child cruelty. According to the father's attorney, the mother had been lying about the abuse. Now the boy's father wondered whether she was lying again, as well as encouraging his children to lie.

The accused family does have a history of litigation. In 2001 the accused boy's mother sued J.C. Penney, claiming security guards at one of their stores beat her, the boy and his brother after they left the store with unpaid merchandise, and that the store officials had sexually assaulted her. That case was settled for $137,500.

Those close to the boy's family say that when Michael Jackson became alarmed that the BBC documentary with Martin Bashir might make Michael appear to be a pedophile, he then banned the boy and his mother from the Neverland Ranch. Michael also tried to make them leave town.

Michael Jackson's lawyers have challenged the indictment on the grounds that the extreme secrecy surrounding the grand jury hearings intimidated the jurors into handing down the indictment.

By this time I was nothing more than an advisor: a figurehead at the head of the formerly powerful MJJ Communications and Production Company. And on a sunny November day, cuffed and stuffed in the back of an unmarked police cruiser, Michael was disgracefully back on the world stage.

On live television, the world would witness the fall of the King of Pop.

Bob Jones was standing about fifty feet away from Michael on the day of the January 2004 arraignment when, inexplicably, Michael did his now-infamous dance atop a SUV.

Throughout the entire arraignment, in which he showed up twenty minutes late and was chastised by judge for doing so, Michael lacked any hint of seriousness or regard for the situation's gravity.

*It was more apparent than ever that Michael had become delu-
sional. He seemed to think the 2,000 or so fans and hordes of
media in attendance at the arraignment were gathered for a concert rather than a criminal proceeding. The entire day was nothing short of a circus.*

For Michael Jackson, the first indication that this appearance would be different from most came when he realized
there would be no sound check, wrote MSNBC's Michael
Ventre. (For the uninitiated, it is that prelude to a performance
before fans arrive, when the technicians check the levels and
make sure all the equipment is working properly.)

Before this, he indicated to a documentary filmmaker how
mystified he is that anyone would question his habit of sleeping with young boys. He told "60 Minutes" that he was
roughed up during his booking process in Santa Barbara, even
though his demeanor was perky afterward, and audio tapes of
the event suggested the Gloved One was treated with kid
gloves.

He also told CBS News' Ed Bradley that he was repulsed by
the police search at Neverland Ranch and would have trouble
returning to it; after his court appearance his handlers passed
out invitations to fans for a party there on Friday.

This is all a show. And in any good show, the star performer
likes to keep his fans guessing.

Busses in the "Caravan of Love" brought supporters from
Los Angeles and Las Vegas. Security personnel from the Nation
of Islam stood guard. Members of the singer's family were
there. Reporters from all over the world joined in.

You could feel the excitement. If it is proved that this man
is indeed a child molester, then he'll certainly have a lot of visitors and pen pals while in prison.

It appears that when Michael Jackson faces the music, his
fans are guaranteed to get their money's worth.

The importance of the proceedings was further downplayed as Michael invited all the fans, his family and celebrity B-listers to Neverland for an after party.

I wanted no part of that fiasco. I went straight back to Los Angeles. A party? To celebrate what? His arraignment? I mean, come on, give me a break.

Michael seemed destined, if not determined, to bring about his own destruction. And although not yet convicted, Sheriff Anderson's words ("An arrest warrant for Michael Jackson ...") put an end to a major chapter in Michael's career and began yet another media blitz.

With an ego as large as anyone in popular entertainment has ever seen, Michael has gone from an immensely talented, black icon to a perpetually childlike, wan, genderless, delusional person. His life—regardless of this latest trial's outcome —will never be the same.

2

From Fort Worth to Hollywood

*"Hollywood is the beginning, middle or end
of the universe depending whether you are
a tourist, star wanna-be, or resident."*

—Chamber of Commerce Website

*"Bob Jones is the most loyal and
honest person I've ever known."*

—Michael Jackson, speaking for the
1995 Black Entertainment Television special,
"Bob Jones: Godfather of Black Hollywood"

Just over thirty miles from Dallas, Fort Worth was founded in 1849 as one of ten forts along the Texas frontier. By 1853 the frontier had moved further west and the military abandoned the fort. Taken over by settlers, it became a town.

Within a few decades, and partly because of the town's location as the last major center before the Chisholm Trail, Fort Worth became known as Cow Town. Also, because of its location along the great cattle trails from Texas, Fort Worth spawned Hell's Half Acre: a region of saloons, gambling joints ,and dance halls that attracted cowboys and desperadoes alike.

With the eventual arrival of the railroad, the Fort Worth Stockyards became a premier livestock shipyard and remained

33

so until the 1960s. But cattle only helped to start the city; oil made it grow. When oil wells began to pop up throughout west Texas in the early 1900s, many of the deals were made in Fort Worth, and here much of the money was spent.

Born the son of the late Ruby Faye and Ocie Jones, Bob Jones grew up amid the backdrop of 1940s Fort Worth.

> *I know most people don't want to be bored with the details of my upbringing and I won't bother with much of that, but I will say that my parents were a strong duo who didn't bring me up in poverty.*
>
> *At least in some ways, I was quite fortunate for a black boy in Texas. I was the product of hardworking parents who only wanted what was good for their son. I wasn't trying to disappoint, and I believe I succeeded in* not *disappointing them.*

Jones's father was a dance promoter, booking such acts as Sarah Vaughn, Louis Jordan, Count Basie, and Lionel Hampton. His father's partner in their promotions company was Don Robey, the founder of Peacock Records, a leading rhythm and blues label out of Houston, Texas in those days.

When the Jones family moved to Los Angeles, young Bob Jones gained even greater exposure to the entertainment greats of the day. While a student at Los Angeles High School, he also became an avid reader of Hollywood columnists Louella Parsons, Harrison Carroll, and Mike Connolly of the *Hollywood Reporter.* At age sixteen, he began writing a column for the now defunct *California Eagle* newspaper.

> *I did my own groundwork. I wrote to all of the black newspapers and sent them samples of my column. I wrote about Eartha Kitt, Nat King Cole, and Duke Ellington.*

He studied business education at USC. He remained a big fan of the journalists like Walter Winchell and Louella Parsons. And around him he saw all the Hollywood parties going on without him. At USC Jones was a writer and entertainment editor at the height of the *Herald Dispatch's* publication. After syndicating his Hollywood column to more than eighty black newspapers, a few years later, Jones met entertainer Bobby Darin. They became fast friends, and that association led Jones to his next job as a publicist for Rogers, Cowan & Brenner Public Relations. Earlier, Jones had tried and failed to secure a job at Motown.

Now mind you, I had applied to Motown before going to Rogers and Cowan, and as typical of what we all sometimes go through, I guess I didn't qualify for Motown until after Rogers and Cowan accepted me.

One breezy summer night in 1969 at the Playboy Club, Jones was working a party for James Brown's group, the Dee Felice Trio, which featured jazz vocalist Randy Crawford. Later that evening, Jones, Lola Falana and a large group went to Jack Hansen's private club "The Daisy" on Rodeo Drive.

Motown was hosting a party to introduce a new group from Gary, Indiana. Their first night in Hollywood, the group was called The Jackson Five.

With a number of Motown bigwigs in attendance, a young Michael Jackson crooned "Tobacco Road" and bowled over the attendees with James Brown's "I Got the Feeling." Jermaine played rhythm guitar, Tito was lead guitarist, Jackie provided the vocals and banged on the tambourine, and Marlon was the group's background dancer.

In 1970 Jones joined the Motown family as publicity manager for International Talent Management Company. After moving from Rogers and Cowan to Motown, Jones thought he would never leave the famous company. His responsibilities expanded and he became Executive Director of Press, Publicity, and Artist Relations at Motown Records.

Jones was responsible for all of the early Jackson Five interviews and promotional appearances. He also created and implemented media campaigns for numerous top recording artists, including the Jackson Five, Diana Ross, Stevie Wonder, Lionel Richie, Smokey Robinson, the Supremes, Rick James, the Temptations, the Four Tops, Vanity, the Commodores, DeBarge, Bruce Willis, Jermaine Jackson, and El and Chico DeBarge.

His film and television credits would go on to include "Lady Sings the Blues," "Thank God It's Friday," "Mahogany," and the Motown 25th Anniversary specials for NBC- TV.

Motown was and always will be special to me. It wasn't because everybody was a star; it was because we were all family. Acts such as The Supremes, The Four Tops and, of course, The Jackson Five signified Motown. Smokey Robinson and The Miracles' "Shop Around" was the first in our stable to sell one million albums. They were also the first to appear on "American Bandstand."

For many years, Smokey Robinson was the only artist that Berry Gordy would allow to produce his own work. Although it certainly wasn't a hard and fast rule, in general Berry Gordy assigned specific artists to specific producers. Smokey produced Mary Wells, the Temptations and the Miracles. The incredibly successful producing team of Holland-Dozier-Holland produced the Four Tops and the Supremes. Mickey Stevenson produced Marvin Gaye and the Marvelettes. Clarence Paul produced Stevie Wonder. Martha and the Vandellas were produced by both Mickey Stevenson and Holland-Dozier-Holland. Berry also produced many of his artists on occasion.

In 1963 Motown had six records in the Top 10. In 1964 Smokey Robinson produced "My Guy" by Mary Wells, which also went to #1. Motown reached the #2 spot with the Holland-Dozier-Holland-produced "Dancing in the Street," by Martha and the Vandellas. The label certainly deserved the title painted on the front of their headquarters at 2648 West Grand

Boulevard, "Hitsville, USA, The Motown Sound, The Sound of Young America."

In 1966 Motown signed Gladys Knight and the Pips, a group from Atlanta, Georgia, to the Soul label. It was a journeyman group that had hit in 1961 with "Every Beat of My Heart" on the Vee Jay and Fury labels. They were assigned to a young producer named Norman Whitfield. He had recorded Marvin Gaye on a song that Whitfield and Barrett Strong had written called "I Heard It through the Grapevine."

When Berry Gordy refused to release the Marvin Gaye version of the song, Whitfield recorded it with Gladys Knight and the Pips, and the song went to #2. Gladys Knight and the Pips stayed with Motown for seven years, and had a few more hits. (Their biggest hit came after leaving Motown, when they reached #1 with "Midnight Train to Georgia" on the Buddha label.)

When the Marvin Gaye version of "I Heard It through the Grapevine" was finally released later on an album in 1968, the Whitfield-produced song immediately got airplay, forcing its release as a single. The song went all the way to #1, and is today remembered as the definitive version of a classic song.

For 1966 Motown produced fourteen songs that made it to the Top 10, including "You Can't Hurry Love" and "You Keep Me Hanging On" by the Supremes. Also in 1966, Norman Whitfield took over production responsibilities for the Temptations from Smokey Robinson. His first production for the Temptations was "Ain't Too Proud to Beg," which he co-wrote with Eddie Holland.

When Whitfield teamed with Barrett Strong to write for the Temptations, the result was a new sound for Motown called "Psychedelic Soul." "Cloud Nine" was just the first of several Whitfield-Strong compositions to go Top 10, including "Run Away Child, Running Wild," the #1 hit "I Can't Get Next To You," "Psychedelic Shack," and Ball of Confusion (That's What the World is Today)."

In 1967 thirteen Motown singles reached the Top 10 charts. "Love is Here and Now You're Gone" and "The Happening" by the Supremes both reached #1. Motown had five major labels active: Motown, Tamla, Gordy, Soul, and V.I.P. And, in a move that would have tremendous significance for the company's future, Berry Gordy purchased a home in Los Angeles, California that year.

A tremendous loss for Motown occurred about that time, when arguably the most successful producers in history, Holland, Dozier, and Holland, left the company. Perhaps the only producers other than Phil Spector to become as big a name as the artists they recorded, the team was forced into inactivity from 1968 to 1970 as a result of lawsuits stemming from their Motown departure.

Holland, Dozier, and Holland established two labels in 1970, Hot Wax and Invictus, and had moderate success with acts such as Chairmen of the Board, Flaming Ember, Freda Payne, and others, but they didn't repeat the kind of hit-after-hit success they had previously enjoyed at Motown.

In its tenth year of operation, 1969, Motown continued to roll along. That year, Bobby Taylor, lead singer with a group called the Vancouvers, brought a singing family from Gary, Indiana, to Berry Gordy's attention.

The Jackson Five were signed to Motown. Four of their first six singles released between late 1969 and mid 1971 went to #1 on the pop charts, with the two that missed the #1 spot reaching #2.

In order to prevent the creation of new superstar producers like Holland-Dozier-Holland, Gordy credited writing and production on Jackson Five records to "The Corporation." This was a team consisting of Berry Gordy, Freddie Perren, Deke Richards and Fonzie Mizell.

In 1969 Motown established the Rare Earth label to issue white psychedelic rock music and other alternatives to R&B.

The West Coast offices of Motown handled the label. Rare Earth also was the name the first group signed to the label, a Detroit group originally formed in 1961 as the Sunliners. Their first album contained a twenty-minute version of the Temptations' hit, "Get Ready" that was produced by Norman Whitfield.

Not too successful, the Rare Earth label limped along until 1976. In 1969, Motown acquired the distribution rights to the Chisa Label, which was founded by Hugh Masekela and Stewart Levine.

In 1970 six of the fourteen Motown singles that reached the Top 10 went to #1. They included "Ain't No Mountain High Enough" by Diana Ross—now without the Supremes. The final performance of Diana Ross and the Supremes had occurred at the Frontier Hotel in Las Vegas, which was recorded and issued as an album. Jean Terrell then replaced Diana Ross as lead singer of the Supremes.

Motown became more cognizant of its roots by establishing a new subsidiary label called Black Forum in 1970, releasing spoken word records by Dr. Martin Luther King, Jr., Stokely Carmichael and black poets Langston Hughes and Margaret Danner. The label was active until 1973.

In 1971 Motown has eleven singles reach the Top 10, with "Just My Imagination (Running Away with Me)" by the Temptations reaching the #1 spot. During this year, Motown also moved expanded into television production. It produced "Diana!" a television special with Diana Ross, and "Goin' Back to Indiana," a Jackson Five special.

A cartoon series about the Jackson Five also started in 1971. A new subsidiary was established called Mowest. Its first release was "What the World Needs Now Is Love/Abraham, Martin, and John": a sweet-sounding medley interspersed with jarring recordings drawn from politically relevant issues such as war and assassination put together by Los Angeles deejay Tom Clay.

The Mowest label was controlled by the West Coast office of Motown and was used for talent developed by that office.

By 1971 Marvin Gaye had been given creative control of his recordings, in that year he made an album titled "What's Going On," for which he wrote, produced, sang and played most of the instruments. At first, Gordy did not want to release the album, feeling that the album's hard-hitting, socially critical lyrics on songs like "Inner City Blues" would offend traditional Motown fans.

Only after Gaye threatened to never make another record for Motown did Gordy relent and release the album. It is often acknowledged as one of the greatest albums ever made. "What's Going On" sold over a million copies and spawned three R&B number one hits, "Mercy Mercy Me (The Ecology)," "What's Going On" and "Inner City Blues (Make Me Wanna Holler)." All three songs also made the popular music Top 10 lists.

The music on the album is spacey, spiritual and soulful, totally different than any album ever released on Motown. With "What's Going On," Gaye had raised Motown music to a new level. It also made album sales a significant factor to a company that had always chased the hit single.

1972 was somewhat of a down year for Motown. Only four singles reaching the pop Top 10. Diana Ross also began her film career with "Lady Sings the Blues," receiving an Academy Award nomination for her portrayal of Billie Holiday.

As the Los Angeles offices continued to grow, the Detroit headquarters shrank. A company newsletter in March 1972 stated, "There are no plans at present to phase out the Detroit operations, as many rumors suggest." However, in June, Motown announced it was closing its Detroit offices and moving its headquarters to Los Angeles.

While the move probably made sense because of Berry Gordy's increasing emphasis on movies and television, many Motown fans believe the company's heart and soul was lost when it abandoned Detroit, that its most creative days were the thirteen years from 1959 to 1972.

In 1973 Berry Gordy resigned as President of Motown Records to become Chairman of the Board of Motown Industries, which included the record, motion picture, television and publishing divisions. Ewart Abner II, a Motown Vice President for six years (and former exec with Vee-Jay) became President of Motown Records.

In 1974 a new group, the Commodores, had their first album released, titled "Machine Gun." It went gold in five countries. In retrospect, the title track, an instrumental, was quite uncharacteristic of the smooth ballads featuring the voice of Lionel Richie that later became the group's mainstay. The Commodores went on to become Motown's best-selling act during the 1970s. For the period of 1974 to 1980, they averaged two million album sales per year.

1975 marked a low point in Motown history, as only one Motown release "Boogie On Reggae Woman" by Stevie Wonder made the Top 10. That year, The Jackson Five left Motown for Epic records. Actually, The Jackson 4 went to Epic as "The Jacksons." Jermaine, who had married Berry Gordy's daughter, stayed with Motown.

Ewart Abner II resigned as President of Motown Records and Berry Gordy temporarily replaced him. Barney Ales, a former Vice President of the company, who had stayed in Detroit when the company moved to Los Angeles, rejoined the company when Motown purchased his Prodigal Label. During the year, Diana Ross starred in her second movie, "Mahogany." It was certainly not as well received as "Lady Sings the Blues."

In 1976 the fortunes of the company rebounded with six Motown releases reaching the Top 10, including two hits by the Commodores. Three of the company's releases reached #1, and Stevie Wonder released his "Songs in the Key of Life" album, which entered the pop charts at #1. He picked up four more Grammys for the album.

Rick James was signed to the Gordy label and his first album "Come and Get It" eventually sold two million copies. James' breakthrough album was 1981's "Street Songs," which sold over three million copies. Motown Pictures produced "The Wiz" starring Diana Ross in 1978.

During the 1980s Motown continued to sell massive numbers of albums, culminating with Lionel Richie's 1984 "Can't Slow Down." It became the largest selling album in the company's history when it sold 10 million copies worldwide.

In 1982 Motown went to a consolidated numbering system for all albums released on the three remaining active labels, Motown, Gordy and Tamla. In addition to the three major labels, Motown also released albums on the Latino label, which was Motown's attempt at a Hispanic label, and Morocco, which stood for Motown Rock Company.

In June 1988 Berry Gordy sold Motown Records to a partnership between MCA and Boston Ventures, with Gordy retaining the ownership of the Jobete Publishing catalog. Always the consummate businessman, and as good as he was as a judge of talent and hit songs, Berry Gordy was foremost an entrepreneur. He transformed an $800 loan into the largest black-owned business in United States history.

In 1976 he pretty much summed it up, saying "I earned 367 million dollars in 16 years. I must be doing something right!"

Even though Motown sold millions more albums during the 1970s and 1980s than it had in the 1960s, Motown will be remembered mostly for the music it created during the 1960s, the songs heard on tinny radios in automobiles as teenagers cruised the streets and highways. Never in history has one company produced so many top ten hits as Motown did during that marvelous decade.

In 1987 Michael Jackson called Bob Jones. Michael asked Jones what it would take to bring him on board to head the communications and media division of MJJ Productions. After getting the okay from Motown founder Berry Gordy, Bob Jones officially parted company with the family he knew as Motown, signing on with the fledgling King of Pop.

The great Motown era was over for Bob Jones, but life in the fastest of fast lanes was about to begin for the Texas-born publicist.

3

Send Me Your Poor, Your Disenfranchised

(However, Please Allow Them to Be White)

"I heard about cats like you, Scared of your
own shadow because it acts like you."

—Da Slim Poet

"Only in America can you be born a black man
and end up a white woman."

—An unidentified journalist

It wasn't until several months after becoming head of MJJ
Communications that I realized how little Michael Jackson
thought of black people. Any time he hired someone or agreed to
work with someone, his excuse for not going with a black candi-
date for the job would always be that he was only seeking the
best qualified—regardless of skin color.

Michael Jackson—beneath the bleached skin that has made
him a grotesque caricature of a female alien—was black too. He
was also the weirdest and most inexplicable of racists.

His favorite word to describe blacks, his original race, was
Splaboo. Yep, Splaboo. It was a word he used a lot, a word he
used around people such as Macaulay Culkin.

I think a 1973 incident in Melbourne, Australia illustrated why Michael kept me on the job. Richard Schmeiszi, a newspaper writer with the Observer, asked Michael how it felt to be born a nigger in America, but still being able to buy the plane he flew to Australia on. Michael told Schmeiszi that he didn't know the answer to that question, but to wait a minute and he would get someone to answer. After Michael filled me in, I calmly informed Schmeiszi that it was a helluva lot better than being born in Australia and put on a reservation in your own country (like many Native Peoples in Australia). After our conversation grew heated, Schmeiszi angrily departed. This exchange made the news the next day, which impressed the hell out of Michael.

Michael's hatred of blacks may have stemmed from his father Joseph, who always favored lighter-skinned black folks. The Jackson family mostly followed Joseph's lead. Jermaine first married Hazel, who was not only lighter-skinned, but was the daughter of Berry Gordy. Tito, Jackie, Janet, and many of the younger generations have selected white or non-blacks as their mates.

Rebbie was the first in the family to marry. She wed a dark-skinned black man, whom the family despised. They had three children, all of the darker persuasion. Michael simply tolerated these kids, but privately despised them simply because of the color of their skin. In contrast, Michael did take a liking to Tito's lighter-skinned sons, as well as Jermaine's.

When Michael's mother Katherine came along on tours, she'd often lament that Michael didn't always have to have those "little white boys" around. He had plenty of nieces and nephews, Katherine would say, to provide any company Michael might need.

Someone once said that Michael Jackson wanted to not only *look* different, but also *be* different from every black man in the universe. He wanted to return to his childhood and relive it as a white boy. What set him apart from your ordinary delusional character was that Michael Jackson did just that.

One of the first things Michael Jackson did to permanently separate himself from his family and the real world, was to purchase Neverland. Of course his worship of Peter Pan led to his naming the 2,700-acre estate "Neverland."

Former Beatle Paul McCartney, then a good friend of Michael Jackson, had Michael come up to Los Olivos, California where the duo filmed the video "Say Say Say." McCartney had considered purchasing the property, but didn't.

When Michael Jackson first offered to buy the property, realtors and neighbors balked. It was stated that they didn't want "his kind" up in the Santa Ynez Valley. But Jackson was determined to acquire the property, which is about two hours from Los Angeles.

If you stand at the gates of Michael's home, it may not be easy at first to tell it apart from any of the other ranches that stretch up the hills of Figueroa Mountain Road in Los Olivos. But Michael added, well, Michael's unique touch. With its cast-iron steel gates painted gold, and a massive crown sitting atop, you knew it was home to royalty, or, at least, wannabe royalty.

Neverland Ranch became Michael's sanctuary from the outside world. It is replete with a menagerie of exotic animals, theme park rides, a movie theater, library, arcade and a host of shrines to Michael's favorite entertainers, including himself.

Neverland is Michael's kingdom. It has the feel of Disneyland, with constantly-playing music piled throughout the estate. It even has its own railroad system and fire department. This bizarre place perfectly fits his lifestyle. In Michael's mind, even other celebrities are viewed as mere common-folk.

Many of the people he sees when leaving and returning to Neverland are cattle ranchers and day laborers. He also has some famous neighbors like Cheryl Ladd and Bo Derek.

The week of February 14, 1988 was significant for Bob Jones. This would be the first time that he'd get to see his boss perform in concert as a solo act.

The rehearsals for the "Bad" concert tour were held in Pensacola, Florida. Security man Bill Bray arranged for me to fly to Florida a few days prior to the show's kickoff in Kansas City's Kemper Arena. This same arena is where Michael and his brothers launched their "Victory" tour four years earlier.

Sony had made elaborate arrangements for a major sendoff to the concert tour. They were making a great effort because "Bad" was Michael's first release since his record-breaking "Thriller" album. This was Michael's first tour since that "Victory" tour with the brothers.

Michael's security guard, Wayne Nagin, led me into his suite at the hotel. I was shocked. Michael Jackson and his brothers were known for their pillow fights while on the road. They also become notorious for trashing hotel rooms. However, in all my years in the business, I had never seen a suite that had been so destroyed by an act.

The chandelier was completely covered with liquid string. Lamps, tables and chairs were thrown about. Food wrappers and all sorts of other garbage covered the floors, tables and bed. The housekeeper had been paid off not to tell.

The Kansas City tour opening proved a great success. We now headed to the Big Apple, where Michael was to make an appearance on the Grammy Awards. Sony hoped this appearance would propel sales of "Bad" the way Michael's electric performance on the "Motown 25 Special" had ignited "Thriller" sales.

What was also notable about our trip to New York was, again, Michael's love of white folks and white celebrity. A who's who list of the rich and famous came to Madison Square Garden to see Michael perform a benefit concert for the United Negro College Fund. Earlier the UNCF had presented the King with an honorary degree at a hotel ceremony. He also received the Frederick D. Patterson Award for his attempts to eliminate world hunger and his work with gravely ill children.

Although Whitney Houston joined the King and Liza Minnelli on the podium when Michael accepted one of his honors, he spent little time with Houston. Instead, he went back to his suite at the Helmsley Palace Hotel, virtually ignoring pop diva Houston while spending much time with lily-white celebrities Minnelli and Taylor.

But humiliation would come just days later for Michael Jackson. Nominated for multiple Grammy Awards, Michael despised being assigned a seat next to Quincy Jones, the producer of his "Thriller" and "Bad" albums. Michael Jackson already thought Quincy had received too much of his spotlight.

Later Quincy would further add to Michael's fury at the Black Radio Exclusive Awards. The great producer was assigned the task of presenting Michael Jackson with an award and Bob Jones was given the task of re-writing Quincy's speech.

I put the words in the speech for Quincy to refer to Michael as "the King of Pop"—a title I had bestowed upon him because Michael had wanted a moniker like Bruce Springsteen, Frank Sinatra and Elvis. In fact, I was the one who got Liz Taylor to introduce him at the Soul Train Awards in 1989 as "the King of Pop, Rock and Soul." Anyway, on this particular night, Quincy read my ghost-written speech, but left out the "King of Pop" part. Michael was furious.

The 1988 Grammys was one of the most boring in memory, brought to life only by Michael's soulful performance of "The Way You Make Me Feel" and "Man in the Mirror." But an upset Jackson stormed out of the show after being shut out of all the awards for which he had been nominated. Lost on Jackson was the fact that hip-hop was that year's real story. The genre was an exploding pop-culture phenomenon.

The fact that Michael's special award wasn't televised and had been relegated to the pre-show portion of the ceremony drew the ire of many and was the focus of some media attention. The duo Fresh Prince and Jazzy Jeff won Best Rap Performance that year, and it was their boycott of the ceremony that sparked controversy and stole all headlines, including those about Jackson's landmark performance.

Then what galled me was that Michael had his black conversation: the conversation where he all of a sudden wanted to be black because he felt victimized. He said he didn't want to do any more of these awards shows or any other television because these racist white people only used him for ratings.

As the "Bad" tour moved to St. Louis, a thirteen-year-old boy named Peter joined the entourage. This kid had been with us in New York and was now coming along for the entire tour. Michael completed the first of three dates in St. Louis, but then complained that he had gotten sick because Peter was sick and the young boy had somehow spread his germs to him. Security man Bill Bray had told the boy's mother to keep the boy away from Michael since the kid had the flu.

Later Peter and his parents went to Europe with us. The tabloids had a field day with their questions about the boy and his parents. One tabloid reported that Michael had purchased the kid by giving the parents a Rolls Royce. To the best of my knowledge, that did not happen. However, it would not have surprised me. Things were getting weird.

(Steve Chabre, a former President of MJJ Enterprises, later told me that Michael did purchase a luxury automobile for this family, as well as a house in the San Fernando Valley in California— all without informing his lawyer or accountants.)

Bill Bray told me that Sam's father worked for a rubbish collection service, but the father nevertheless stayed on the road with us the entire tour. And on its every stop, Michael and Peter stayed locked in Michael's suite.

Bray told the staff to keep the parents of the boy occupied: take them shopping, on trips, just keep them busy doing something, anything! I remember getting an approval from Bill Bray to throw an elegant birthday dinner party for the boy's mother at the exclusive Hotel Negresco, one of the most expensive hotels in the world. The King didn't bat an eye at the huge bill the party rang up. After all, we had the boys' parents with us and we did whatever it took to keep them occupied.

Whatever social or business obligations Michael had, the parents and the boy had to be included. It was law. He wouldn't accept invitations if he couldn't bring that family.

One of the oddest things that happened occurred at Paris' DeCrillion Hotel. Jolie Levine, Jackson's assistant at the time found a bed sheet in the King's hotel bedroom. On it, Michael had drawn a picture of the Peter and himself. Also written on the sheet was what amounted to a love note to the boy. Worried that if a hotel housekeeper got a hold of the sheet, it could end up in the hands of the media or law enforcement, we had our secretary pack it, taking it with us. That sheet was my first tangible clue that Michael Jackson, the King of Pop, was up to no good with this young kid.

Of course, before then I had heard some suggestive stories. You know, like the stories about Emmanuel Lewis and the baby bottles. Pictures of Emmanuel and Michael sucking baby bottles were published in April 2005 in In Touch magazine. Stories that Michael wasn't asexual as some thought, or that he wasn't necessarily homosexual. However, what most of these stories did seem to suggest was that Michael was interested in little boys.

The drawing on the bed sheet along with the love note was a definite cause for concern. I was told that in Nice, Michael Jackson's manager Frank Dileo found a sheet painted with human feces.

True, one of Michael's favorite terms had always been "doo-doo," but I didn't think he took such a literal interest.

It was during the "Bad" tour that Michael's friend Eddie Murphy introduced Jackson by way of Farrakhan's tapes to the orations of Nation of Islam Minister Louis Farrakhan. That was interesting in as much as Farrakhan had blasted Jackson in a 1984 *People* magazine interview. At the time, the minister had also called for a boycott of the "Victory" tour.

This is how the famous Nation of Islam Minister described Jackson: "He's a bad role model. His Jehri-curl, female acting, sissified-acting expression is not wholesome for our young boys, or our young girls."

I provided seats for the Minister during the Chicago stop on the "Bad" tour. Eddie Murphy had given Michael some of the minister's speeches after Michael claimed an interest. After the Chicago show, the Minister was so impressed with the performance that he proclaimed Michael a "Special Messenger of Entertainment." He literally raved about Michael's artistry and often praised him in subsequent speeches.

Later, the Minister would come to better understand Michael. That was around the time Michael understood that black people could be useful for certain tasks. You see, the King hated using blacks for anything. Few people know that Michael was the single biggest contributor to Farrakhan's Million Man March. Michael gave Farrakhan $25,000.

Evvy, Michael's secretary, delivered the money to me in $100 bills; it was done that way because I didn't want Michael's donation to be directly tied to him if the shit should happen to hit the fan. I made them give me a receipt for the money in my name. I still have that receipt.

This is how Michael operated: always willing to hang someone else out to dry and cover his own ass. You see, if the media and public found out that Michael Jackson donated anything to an event sponsored by the Nation of Islam, he'd lose his Jewish friends and a lot of his fan base would turn against him. But Michael did what Michael wanted to do.

The reason for Michael's generosity? Well, the King had run into a problem with some Hollywood heavyweights. Five of them to be exact. In return for Michael's contribution to the Million Man March, I was to ensure that the Minister made mention of the "persecution" Michael was suffering following the release of the song "They Don't Care About Us." The song had drawn much criticism because of these lyrics:

"Jew me, Sue me, everybody do me. Kick me kike me, don't you black or white me."

Michael now wanted to start a kind of holy war by publicly admonishing these executive Jews for the problems they created by objecting to those lyrics.

The Minister is not a foolish man. Having now heard of Michael's reputation for turning on anyone at the drop of a hat, he wasn't about to get involved with Michael. With the King, you never knew: he just might not speak to you the next time he saw you.

Farrakhan would later mention Michael in a speech, but he didn't attempt to antagonize people like Steven Spielberg, Jeffrey Katzenberg, David Geffen, Michael Milkin and Steve Wynn. Michael had long trumpeted his "friendship" with these gentlemen but had noticed that, in his dire time of need, during these accusations of anti-Semitism, they were not in his corner. More on this later in the book.

Jesse Jackson's son was running for a Congressional seat and had sought Michael for financial assistance. Michael agreed to offer support but only on the basis that the Reverend Jackson would slam his Jewish friends.

Michael's anger blazed even hotter after the March, when he proclaimed to us that he had been double-crossed by the minister and others.

When Minister Farrakhan spoke at the march he referred to Jews as "financial bloodsuckers." However, Farrakhan's speech disappointed Michael. Reverend Farrakhan said: "… So you whitened up religion, Farrakhan didn't do that. You locked the Bible from us. Farrakhan didn't do that."

Farrakhan went onto talk about the "sick minds: some who wouldn't even let you bury us in the same ground that both of us came out of. We had to be buried somewhere else, that's sick."

He said "some blacks died just to drink water out of a fountain marked 'White.' That's sick. Isn't it sick?" He spoke of how religion had been poisoned. And in all the churches, until recently, the master was painted white.

And Farrakhan spoke of how he thought blacks were used by major universities and pro sports owners. "Then they find themselves with your daughter. Then you take them into the NBA, the NFL and they become megastars. Or in the entertainment field and when they become megastars, their associations are no longer black. They may not have a black manager, a black agent, a black accountant."

Finally he mentioned the King. "I'm not degrading my brother; I love him. But he was drawn out. He didn't sell out; he was drawn out. Michael Jackson is drawn out."

Stevie Wonder, however, a Motown alumnus with Jackson, spoke of the common suffering of Jews and blacks. In fact, Wonder all but called for the unity of Jews and Blacks by saying "All for one, one for all."

The firestorm over Michael's lyrics also impacted me. We went to Brazil to shoot the song's video. We were filming in the Flavalas, the dismal home to many poor people. Now the King doesn't like blacks and these people were dark. Still, Michael was trying to make a point by using the poor and dark of Brazil.

However, to further underscore his mindset when it comes to blacks, Michael wanted to paint some middle class Italian kids and use them in the video. Director Spike Lee had to talk him out of it, telling the King that he'd be run out of Rio if he did such a thing.

One of the kids he wanted to paint was Frank Cascio (who later became known as Frank Tyson). Frank would become an important cog in the Jackson wheel, though back then he was just a young teenager whom Michael was very fond of.

I know that Michael began taking care of this family, who were from New Jersey. Cascio's father was Dominick Cascio, the Towers Manager at the New York's Helmsley Palace Hotel. Dominick worked closely with security man Bill Bray on whatever things that needed arranging whenever the King stayed at the Helmsley.

Dominick and his wife, Connie, who also became an "advisor" to the King, would come on the road with us. Also along for the ride were their three sons, including Frank, who would always stay in the suite with Michael.

I believe I was asked to leave Eastern Europe and go back to the States early because of a nasty confrontation I had with Michael Jackson over the impropriety of having these boys staying in his hotel suite.

Connie, who had absolutely no experience or training in show business, advised Michael on many matters. Although Michael had a mother, he always seemed to be looking for another mother figure, or someone with feminine instincts to help guide him.

Frank later became Michael's errand boy and did everything the King asked of him. You know something? The King did everything Frank wanted him to do as well. It became even weirder in Jacksonville. For me, Neverland had become I-never-want-to-go-there-land.

Michael's relationship with Frank Cascio grew. He adored the young fellow. Michael even had clothes made for Cascio so that the youngster would look just like him. Michael Jackson would even cancel business meetings if Frank instead wanted to go to Disneyland or just play with water guns or just sleep in. Again, what was wrong with these parents?

Most in the camp always thought of Michael as asexual. So, I was beginning to wonder about what was going on. Was this asexual thing just a front for some sinister behavior on the king's part?

Researchers have asserted that there exists a large degree of variation in the experiences of asexual people. It also suggests that the underlying causes of their lack of sexual attraction may be drastically different. Some asexuals might simply have extreme low sex drives in spite of an innate orientation toward males or females. Other asexuals might form a category of sexual orientation in addition to the hetero-, homo, and bi-sexual ones, namely people who are attracted to neither gender, even if they have normal sex drives.

Well, it started to seem to me that Michael did indeed have some sort of sexual drive and it wasn't the least bit natural. In addition to the kid from the "Bad" tour, there was another boy whom he had a keen interest in. This kid, Damon Patrick, was a favorite of Michael's.

This boy's mom would often complain to Bill Bray. She'd be asking to see her own child, trying to get a security man to convince Michael to let her see her own son. It was said, and I have no concrete proof, that Michael paid several million dollars to Damon Patrick's family once that affair was over.

This same family also came on the road with us. Michael picked up the tab for all of them, including a tutor for the young boy. That tutor had to be one of the happiest people on earth because he was rarely called upon to do any work. The boy was always with Michael and didn't have time for school.

Michael's children sidekicks ranged from the anonymous to the famous. At this point, some of Michael's choices seemed to suggest massive recklessness and immaturity on his part. Everybody sympathized with Michael's seemingly innocent attempts to experience a childhood that he claims never to have had.

But who can forget Michael's oddball attendance at the 1984 Grammy Awards, the night he swept the awards because of the "Thriller" success? Brooke Shields sat beside him while pint-sized Emmanuel Lewis sat atop his lap.

Most people were astonished upon seeing strange sights like these. However, raised eyebrows turned to heads shaking when, prior to my joining the team, one of Michael's p.r. people had to explain stories like him sleeping in the hyperbaric chamber—supposedly so that he could live forever— and the rumors that Michael wanted to buy the Elephant Man's bones.

Did Michael take dangerous chances? Of course he did. Some have even claimed that it nearly cost him dearly—Mob-style, if you will.

Michael had befriended Miko Brando, son of "The Godfather," Marlon Brando. Miko was supposed to be a security guard, but he was young and the son of Marlon. Bill Bray informed me that the reason Miko had so much freedom was that Michael was very afraid of Marlon.

The King seemed to favor the blond-haired and young. In my experience with Michael, once a boy turned fourteen or fifteen years old, he'd began severing ties. The King did have a saying that has long since stuck with me: "No wenches, bitches, heifers and hoes." This was the sort of terminology he'd use referring to women. He didn't much want them around.

There was at least one exception: Elizabeth Taylor. Because she too had been a child star who developed into an icon, she captured Michael Jackson's imagination—so much so that he built something of a shrine to her at Neverland.

Motown superstar Lionel Richie, when interviewed by author J. Randy Taraborelli, said that one night he, Elizabeth, and Michael Jackson went out to dinner. "Because she was also a child star, Elizabeth Taylor could relate to Michael Jackson. They talked about isolation and what you do when you're lonely. It was good for Michael to hear that Elizabeth often went out of the house without security guards. The idea that you could leave without security guards was a revelation to Michael Jackson."

In 1991 Taylor met Larry Fortensky while in rehab at the Betty Ford Clinic, and she soon planned to marry the construction worker. Michael, wanting to flex his financial muscles, offered to hold the affair at Neverland the ranch.

> He wanted to impress and gave Norma Staikos a million dollars to take care of whatever was needed for the wedding.
>
> Also noteworthy was that Michael didn't invite any of the Jacksons to the event. I didn't get an invite until four days before the gala and that was only because my close friend Chen Sam was Elizabeth's right-hand. Chen had wanted me to attend.
>
> At the wedding, Michael approached and asked me where the John H. Johnsons and Berry Gordys of the world were. I replied that I had nothing to do with this wedding. Hell, I had just received the invite four days prior. I hadn't been allowed to plan or do anything. This was a Norma Staikos production.
>
> It astounds me how Michael's relationship with Elizabeth developed into what it is today. He goes out of his way to buy her the most expensive things and she agrees to appear on television specials on his behalf so long as she's paid.

As one writer put it, what Taylor and Jackson seem to share, more than anything else, is a sense of communality, of being kindred spirits. "He is the least weird man I know," Taylor said of Jackson. "My childhood and Michael's childhood are so similar and so strange," Taylor told Oprah Winfrey. She said she and Michael had no chums their own age and she said she simply "thank God," adored horse riding, which she had for her release. Taylor said she "loved her horse with a total passion. But Michael had nothing!"

Perhaps it was these perceived childhood similarities that drew Taylor to Jackson. Then again, when you have someone like Michael sending Bill Bray to Australia to secure you million-dollar gifts, most would see his appeal. Michael went far out of his way to impress Taylor, including providing her with jewelry and other gifts totaling hundreds of thousands of dollars.

If things weren't weird enough for Bob Jones, he was about to encounter a situation that made his most famous boss appear as the oddball of the century.

Bob Jones, Randy Jackson and Michael Jackson entertain Temptations singer Eddie Kendricks at the Jacksons California compound during a family Thank You party. Jones says Kendricks was one of the nicest people show business has ever seen.

Michael Jackson holds a boomerang as he and his brothers greet the locals on the Jacksons first trip to Australia.

At a Motown Records gathering, (from l to r) Bob Jones, Marvin Gaye and Smokey Robinson.

Bob Jones and Michael Jackson share a moment with Jackson school tutor Rose Fine.

Bob Jones dines with Marlon Jackson, Michael Jackson, Rose Fine and Lester Morney, tour publicist, during the Commodores concert tour.

Bob Jones backstage with the late Grover Washington Jr.

Taking a break from the Bad tour, Michael Jackson goofs around at Disneyland

During a break in a concert tour, Michael Jackson finds solace on a playground in Germany.

Michael Jackson and security chief Bill Bray observe their surroundings in Germany

Michael Jackson reclines with some youngsters he met at the Children's Museum in Washington, DC. Jackson was feted by President George H.W. Bush on this trip for his work with children.

Bob Jones yuks it up with author Adrian Grant. It was Grant's "Visual Documentary" book that Jones says helped him recall a lot of the details in this book.

Bob Jones with another of his famous clients, singer Vanity.

4

The Honeymoon

"Love will make you do wrong, will make you do right."

—Al Green, Love & Happiness

*"Whatever we do whatever we say now
we'll make a vow to keep it in the closet."*

—Michael Jackson from the 1993 single "Keep It in the Closet"

Hardly a day went by at MJJ Communications that Bob Jones didn't find himself fending off media inquiries about this Michael rumor or that Michael rumor. It was all going wrong now. Really wrong. It became increasingly difficult to understand why young pre-pubescent girls had ever gone mad over Michael Jackson. Or how a vast number of the record-buying public had religiously followed Michael Jackson. Or why the powers-that-be over at Sony Music salivated at their perceived money-making machine.

Jackson had changed. His image was quickly becoming a major obstacle to record sales. His value as a pitchman for products like Pepsi declined even faster.

The traditional techniques of promoting Jackson's image—planting stories of charitable contributions, visiting the young and sick in hospitals, etc.—had become exhausting. More than that, these techniques were no longer effective.

Michael was becoming an outcast. But at this time, Bob Jones still couldn't say whether he thought Jackson was a pedophile. Comparing the known characteristics of pedophiles and holding them next to Jackson still didn't yield a clear-cut answer.

Pedophiles generally don't have criminal records. Well, that fit the King.

Some are professional. Well, the King is a professional pop star.

Some prefer girls. So, not the King.

Some prefer boys. Definitely one of the King's traits.

But experts say pedophiles don't discriminate by race, class, or age. The King discriminates!

One of Michael's security guards, Wayne Nagin, once told me that he and Bill Bray had purchased baby bottles and nipples when Emmanuel Lewis, the little star of "Webster," would visit the King.

Photos of the King and Emmanuel Lewis lying in bed and sucking on baby bottles were published in March 2005 by In Touch Weekly, *a tabloid magazine.*

This brings to mind a memorable trip to Bermuda taken around the time of the King's "courtship" of Macauley Culkin. The King wanted to impress Mac, as he likes to impress everyone, with the fact that he is so sought after by the media. He wanted to demonstrate to Mac that he was so popular that people would go wild for him no matter where he'd go.

To prove this point, we had to bang the drums, if you will, to create a stir without necessarily letting anyone know that the furor had been fabricated within our own camp.

Lee Solters, one of Jackson's publicists assisting me, however, made the mistake of contacting the Public Relations Department of the hotel where the Culkins were staying, and they told Mac's nanny about our mini-p.r. campaign.

Businessman and politician Ross Perot called us and offered to take the King and Mac on a speedboat ride to his estate, as did

*producer Robert Stigwood. The invitation from Perot was accept-
ed. However, Michael declined to go to the Stigwood estate.*

*After we left Bermuda, it was off to Disney World, where we
spent several days before returning to Los Angeles. The King and
Mac flew in a private jet while the rest of us flew by commercial
carrier.*

*I didn't meet Mac until the King filmed his "Black or White"
video. Incidentally, Mac's traveling chaperone in Bermuda was
quite strict and would not allow the King and Mac to sleep together in Michael's suite. This didn't sit well with the King, something
Michael made a point of mentioning to me.*

The year 1993 had started innocently enough, with MJJ trying an image makeover. Once seldom seen, Jackson now began
appearing everywhere. He appeared at the NAACP Image
Awards, the American Music Awards (where Janet Jackson presented him with the Legends Award), The Grammy Awards,
Soul Train Awards, the Super Bowl, and he gave his much-
hyped interview to Oprah Winfrey. "People have been wondering where have I been," Michael said at the Grammy
Awards that year. "Now, I guess they are saying, there he is
again."

Even Jackson had to acknowledge how strange and isolated
he had become. While some saw the various public appearances as simply Jackson being desperate to sell his latest album,
"Dangerous," others were hopeful that this more visible,
touchable, communicative Jackson would become the norm.
But whatever good karma Jackson had rebuilt with an already
dwindling audience and fan base, he was suddenly in danger of
losing.

After Jackson's car broke down in West Los Angeles one
May afternoon, one of the owners of a Rent-a-Wreck shop
pulled off the road to offer assistance. Much to his surprise, the
man noticed the King, and they returned to his shop. Once

there, the man phoned his wife, June and alerted her that Michael Jackson was at Rent-a-Wreck. She rushed over, bringing her daughter and 12-year-old son. Michael Jackson was immediately smitten with the young boy.

The Rent-a-Wreck family and Jackson decided to keep in touch. The King began phoning to speak with the family's twelve-year-old son. They had instantly hit it off. Suddenly, this boy was ubiquitous. Michael showered him with all sorts of gifts, as well as trips to places like Disneyworld and Las Vegas.

What remains incomprehensible to me is how mother June refused to see a problem with just how close Michael had become to her son. Perhaps she was overly smitten with all the shopping sprees and other expensive gifts Michael was providing her.

I first met this family on May 8, 1993 when we were flying to Monaco for the World Music Awards.

Before this trip, I had several conversations with the King's managers Sandy Gallin and Jim Morey, neither of whom ever had any intention of going along. Both had other obligations and had insisted that he not go either.

What was weird was that Morey continued to advise me that Michael would also not be attending the awards because he had too much other business that needed attention.

However, Michael kept whispering to me that we were definitely going to Monaco. Naturally, we did just as the King said we would.

We didn't use the airline tickets provided by the World Music Awards since the King was bringing along his very special guest, the young boy from the Rent-a-Wreck Family.

Norma Staikos had informed me that upon my arrival at LAX airport, I should stand out front of the Bradley International Terminal and wait for an Air France Travel Consultant.

After handling our check-in, the travel agency had arranged for the King to enter the plane from the tarmac. Michael didn't want security man Bill Bray's informants to let him know that we had left the city.

About five minutes prior to departure, the King appeared. He and his guests sat together while I took another seat in another area of the plane. I didn't want Michael to think that I was trying to intrude.

Our flight itinerary was from Los Angeles to Paris, then onto Nice. It was raining upon our arrival in Paris and the pilot had to reassure the King that it was okay to proceed onward.

Michael has a fear of flying. He especially hated to fly at night or when there was any hint of bad weather.

Michael and the young boy were hugging and very close on the plane. They held hands and Michael lovingly gazed into the boy's eyes much like a man would gaze into the eyes of a woman he's in love with. He'd kiss him on the cheek, rub his arms, pet him and inexplicably lick the boy's head.

Upon arrival in Nice, we were met by awards show producer Gary Pudney, and then whisked away in vans to a local heliport. From there, a chopper took us on the ten-minute journey to Monaco.

The King's agreement with the trip's organizers stipulated that the location where he was staying would be disseminated to all, so as to incite fan and media interest. He loved the attention. Hundreds of fans and media greeted us as we arrived at the Hotel de Paris. But many were wondering who the special little guest was that the King had in tow.

We were taken to the Winston Churchill Suite, the King's quarters during his visit. A lovely three-bedroom suite, it had two balconies overlooking the Mediterranean. Once Michael was settled, I went to my suite on another floor. Although not nearly as lavish, I did receive some deluxe provisions, including the champagne Cristal and caviar Beluga.

I instructed the hotel staff that Michael would not accept any calls and that if anyone called for him, they were to be put through to June's room, as per Michael's instructions. Hell, even I now had to call June to get through to Michael.

The show's organizers and producers had put together quite a social calendar for the King. There was a reception at the Loews

Hotel featuring Boys II Men and Prince Albert; a visit to the palace with Prince Albert; dinner at Le Pirate, one of the world's most expensive restaurants; and other functions.

Typically, the King pleaded jet lag, attending just the Loews Hotel event—and that for just thirty minutes. Most of the trip, he stayed in his room with the young boy.

Michael again claimed he had the flu. Even People magazine reported "the flu-stricken Jackson left his hotel suite only twice ..." I arranged for a doctor to visit with Michael and for prescription drugs to be bought in. While I took the doctor to the suite, I stayed in the living room as the doctor examined the King and the young boy in the bedroom.

While this was going on, June was off to San Remo shopping. Norma said they didn't need money because they had already been given $5,000 for expenses and clothes for the kids to wear at the upcoming awards show.

Michael's wooing of the young boy from Rent-a-Wreck was embarrassing: the cooing, hugging, and holding hands. Many of the hotel staff were whispering things such as: "They may as well kiss," or "Did we miss the wedding?" It was shameful, yet to Michael, it was normal behavior. I would later name the trip "The Honeymoon" because it was apparent that Michael Jackson was honeymooning with the boy.

They spent their days and nights locked in the hotel suite they shared while June and her daughter kept busy shopping and doing other things. Michael told me to do whatever she wanted, just as long as she stayed away from him and the boy. It was amazingly sad to see that Michael and this little boy were, dare I say it, in love.

Was it just Michael's big heart and charitable conscious that kept him holed up with the boy and resulted in showing the kid all this affection? I'll never know but, as I told Michael, it was uncomfortable and unfortunate.

One of Michael's standard tactics was to make a play for sympathy. For example, he was to perform at the Soul Train Music

Awards, for which he neither rehearsed nor prepared properly. He really didn't want to do it. When he took the stage to accept an award, he was on crutches. He claimed to have broken his ankle practicing a spin at home.

In this case, Bill Bray had already intimated to me that Michael was faking his injury. I guess in those early days, I was still a little too naïve to realize to what lengths Michael would go to manipulate any given situation while attracting attention.

I will never forget Patti LaBelle saying how much of a trouper the King was when she announced that, even though he had hurt his ankle, he was still going to perform. He performed in a chair.

Later, when he returned home, I was told that he tossed the crutches in front of the 12-year-old boy as soon as he got out the car.

At the World Music Awards, I sat June and the boy together. Actress Linda Evans was seated next to the King. Well, it wasn't long before my seating arrangements were changed and the boy and the King were in each other's arms. I looked on in amazement at what was going on with the King and the boy. Others looked at them askance as well. They held each other tightly, almost in a romantic sense, cooing. There were pecks on the cheeks and on top of the head.

As head public relations man for Michael Jackson, the relationship with the young boy deeply frustrated Bob Jones. And Jones knew the questions from the media would only intensify with each sighting of Jackson and the young boy holding hands.

Alleged pedophilia aside, Michael didn't do himself any p.r. favors with the repeated changes in his appearance. The regular injections of a bleaching agent to whiten his skin were both unbelievable and ungodly.

It made sense only in that he hated dark-skinned and black people. He wanted to be white. I had no doubt about it.

With Michael's obsession with his looks and his compulsive shopping sprees, his debt continued to mount. He was over-the-top. His extreme lifestyle is compounded by the fact that he acts out his fears and anxieties in an extreme fashion.

Michael later invited the Rent-a-Wreck family to accompany him to the Guinness Museum of World Records in Hollywood where the King had to approve a wax statute of him, which was to be unveiled upon our return from the World Music Awards.

After that, Michael found himself in major trouble.

It was August of 1993 and we were scheduled to head overseas to Bangkok, Thailand for the second leg of the "Dangerous" world tour. The bad news broke fast, but Michael and his private investigator Anthony Pellicano had fled the country before the media got wind of the shocking news.

"Pop star Michael Jackson is the subject of a criminal investigation by the Los Angeles Police Department." That was how most of the newscasts led their broadcasts. I had predicted that this relationship was going to cost Michael a lot of money, but it now appeared that it could send the King to jail.

Pellicano had been tipped off ahead of time about the police raids on Neverland and Michael's other properties, so he hurried the King out of the country ahead of the rest of us. The funny thing about the whole mess was that none of us supposed insiders flying to Thailand knew anything about what was going on. However, when our plane landed in Tokyo to refuel, we saw the local news and newspapers, their headlines blaring about Neverland being raided.

Only Norma Staikos was in the know. We later came to understand that Michael, Anthony Pellicano, the boy and the boy's father had been having meetings trying to keep everything quiet. Obviously, those meetings didn't result in any kind of settlement.

Anthony Pellicano addressed the matter on television, saying there was no truth to the allegations that Michael had sexually *molested the boy. Pellicano told news reporters who had gathered for a press conference that Michael Jackson had been presented with a demand for $20 million. When Michael refused to pay, a complaint of child molestation charges was made to Los Angeles' Department of Child and Family Services.*

The "Dangerous" tour was doomed from the start. Michael was in no condition to do the shows and drugs became an issue.

The King wanted Elizabeth Taylor to join him in Singapore. She did.

After canceling many concerts along the way, some of his family met up with Michael in Taipei, Taiwan, where we had a stop. When the Jacksons arrived, they stayed in the same hotel as Michael, Elizabeth Taylor, and her husband Larry Fortensky. Michael didn't want his mother Katherine to come over, but she eventually did, along with Rebbie and Jermaine. She was angry too. "I'm his mother, not Elizabeth Taylor," is what Katherine would later say.

Meanwhile, Michael's shows went on for a while, many being strictly a lip-synch performance. Finally, he was taken to one of Elizabeth Taylor's homes in Gstaad, Switzerland, where her security team could be used. That was notable because, while the King paid $300,000 to $400,000 for international flights and security, Elizabeth's Swiss guards were paid just $100 per day.

Jackson's lawyers finally revealed to the media that he was undergoing six-to-eight weeks of treatment for addiction to painkillers. They would not reveal his location. However, any treatment being done was at the home of Elizabeth Taylor. The subterfuge seemed to be working when media reports had Jackson being spotted in various locations other than Switzerland.

However, a camera crew spotted Michael and Taylor deplaning together in Europe. The frenzied media search continued. There were reported sightings in the French Alps.

Jackson's attorneys Howard Weitzman and Bert Fields continued to portray him as the victim of an extortion attempt. They kept denying that he was staying overseas to avoid arrest.

This was, as one might suspect, the craziest time I'd ever had on the job. We were instructed to give strict no-comments to any and all media inquiries.

Norma Staikos was long gone to Greece when the authorities were hot to talk with her.

The ultra-crazy world of Michael Jackson and the even crazier world of maintaining Jackson's public image had begun to crumble. There had been many previous indications to Bob Jones that something of this sort might occur.

Jackson had left in advance of his world tour, but he left a country on fire. The media was on a desperate search for the details of the 12-year-old boy's accusations. The frenzy hit staggering heights as attorneys, private eyes, law enforcement officials and even doctors took to the television and radio airwaves talking almost non-stop about the accusations. Fuel was further added when in September 1993, the boy filed a civil lawsuit against Jackson, charging him of sexual battery.

The National Enquirer published an exclusive interview with the boy, quoting him as saying "I imagine Michael Jackson is pretty scared right now, really scared. And he should be, because what he did to me is a really bad thing."

In his deposition, the boy says that at first, they slept together with no contact. Michael Jackson then progressed to kissing and putting his tongue in his mouth. When the boy protested, Jackson began to cry, telling him that another friend saw nothing wrong with it. "Michael Jackson said that I did not love him as much as this other friend," said the boy.

1. Their sexual relationship gradually intensified until he claimed: "Michael Jackson masturbated me many times

both with his hand and with his mouth." Jackson, he said, told him "that I should not tell anyone what had happened. He said this was a secret." Jackson told him he had to repeat six wishes three times a day for them to come true:

1. No wenches, bitches, heifers or hoes,

2. Never give up your "bliss,"

3. Live with me in Neverland forever,

4. No conditioning,

5. Never grow up,

6. Be better than best friends forever.

As team Jackson toured the world in support of the "Dangerous" CD, the camp steadfastly avoided acknowledging the accusations. The tour and the circumstances grew even stranger as photographs appeared of Jackson with young boys traveling with him on the tour were shown worldwide. Media everywhere were starting to publish these photos. Michael Jackson was even photographed holding a copy of a magazine with a little boy on the front cover.

Oh, he was doing his thing, but he was scared.

After much behind the scenes negotiating with prosecutors, Jackson decided to return home in December.

I had known Johnnie, went to school went him. I knew he was the right man for the job. Bill Bray asked me to reach out to Johnnie and he came aboard. I don't know what the conversations were between Johnnie and Los Angeles District Attorney Gil Garcetti, but they obviously went well for Michael Jackson.

While an arrest didn't occur, the authorities did something almost as humiliating. They strip searched Jackson and photographed his genitals. "It was the most humiliating experience of my life," Jackson said at the time. "A horrifying nightmare, but if this is what I have to endure to prove my innocence, my complete innocence, so be it."

The boy had drawn a detailed picture showing mottled marks on Jackson's testicles and a dark spot on his left buttock. California prosecutors agreed not to arrest and handcuff Jackson if he agreed to come in and have his genitals photographed. The boy turned out to have an unerring eye for accuracy.

Blanca Francia, a former maid, told a lawyer and testified in the current trial that she had once found Michael in a sleeping bag with her son, and that many times she had seen him nude with young boys. Blanca has now made the same claims on the witness stand in Michael's current case.

Police investigators discovered that Michael surrounded himself with boys between eight and twelve years old, and who were swiftly shown the door as soon as they sprouted any facial hair. But none of the children would testify. Some, like the maid's son, had already been bought off with large sums of money. Other families were threatened to keep silent.

In January 1994 the (recently deceased) ever-savvy Johnnie Cochran engineered a career-saving settlement between Jackson and the Rent-a-Wreck boy. The agreement called for him to receive about $15.3 million in cash. His parents each got $1.5 million and $5 million more went to the boy's lawyer. Before the state could conclude their investigation or lay charges, the family settled with Jackson. The boy, as per the agreement, refused to testify against Michael and under California law at the time, he could not be compelled to do so.

The National Enquirer reported on Michael Jackson's habit of throwing money at problems. The magazine said Michael offered his sister LaToya Jackson money not to publish her unflattering book about the family and tried to get a copy of the book's galleys before its publication.

He did the same with author J. Randy Taraborrelli, who in 1991 wrote the unauthorized biography *Michael Jackson: The Magic and the Madness*. Bart Andrews, Taraborrelli's literary agent, told the news media that Michael Jackson had offered just under $2 million to have the author pull the book from publication. Taraborrelli refused. According to Bart Andrews, Taraborelli stated that he wouldn't be bought off.

Like LaToya's, Taraborelli's book revealed that Joseph Jackson had administered many savage beatings to his boys, but that he was especially brutal to Michael. The book also explored Michael's odd relationship with Emmanuel Lewis, television's "Webster." Lewis' mother put an abrupt halt to that relationship when she discovered that Michael and Emmanuel had checked into a hotel as father and son.

The book further disclosed that Michael was traumatized at age 15 when a family member brought two prostitutes into his hotel room and locked the door on all three of them. Neither the call girls nor Michael had ever discussed the incident, but the book posed an educated guess that Michael was still a virgin where women were concerned.

The situation remained tense around our camp, especially because we knew that the statute of limitations wouldn't run out on this investigation for seven years. We knew these investigators would be watching like hawks.

The settlement virtually guaranteed that Michael Jackson would not be indicted or prosecuted since the agreement stipulated that the young boy would not testify against Jackson. Prosecutors eventually dismissed the Grand Jury and formal charges were never filed.

In 1998, while working as a reporter this book's co-author Stacy Brown interviewed then Santa Clarita, California District Attorney Terry White, who sat in on the 1993 Grand Jury proceedings in Los Angeles. Based on the evidence presented at the

Grand Jury, White said he could state with certainty that there was "more than enough evidence to indict and probably convict Michael Jackson of child molestation."

For several years Michael had to be very careful. People, perhaps prosecutors, were watching him. But his habits didn't change. He still paraded around the globe with little boys. What many people didn't know too was that not only did he pay the Rent-a-Wreck family millions, he had paid a couple of more million to his maid, Blanca. Blanca's son had claimed that something happen between him and the King.

Well, whatever did or did not happen, two million dollars changed hands. These little boys were costing the King millions upon millions.

James Hahn, the current mayor of Los Angeles and back then a city attorney, told a mutual friend of ours that Michael Jackson had better be very, very careful because authorities are watching him and would continue *to watch him.*

For some reason, this brings to mind an encounter Michael Jackson had with the great composer Leonard Bernstein. While I wasn't in the bathroom where this encounter reportedly happened, I was given the intimate details.

For those who are not in tune with the award-winning Bernstein, he was the first American to achieve world-wide recognition as a composer, conductor, pianist, author and teacher. Although he was once married and had children, Bernstein had begun a relationship with a male lover in the 1970s. The relationship was not hidden by Bernstein and the world knew of his preference. But, what was not known was that at some point he apparently grew fond of Michael Jackson.

I was told that after a performance, Bernstein had an encounter with The King in a bathroom. He, I am told, grabbed Michael Jackson and tongue-kissed him passionately. Now, I've never heard Michael speak of it. He certainly didn't say anything

*to me about it and I'm not sure whether or not Michael knew that
I had heard about it.*

*For a man who had always denied homosexuality, yet never
truly showed a penchant for the opposite sex, Michael Jackson was
certainly attracting people other than women.*

5

The King and the Princess

"You look like an angel; you walk like an angel, but I got wise; you're the Devil in disguise."

—Elvis Presley

"Just think, nobody ever thought this would last."

—Michael Jackson, on his marriage to
Lisa Marie Presley at the 1994 MTV Awards

What a union. The daughter of the King of Rock n' Roll, a man everyone initially thought was black, marries the King of Pop, a man many people now think is white.

Media reports around the world focused on how casually Michael and Lisa Marie were dressed for the wedding ceremony. "Michael looked like a little boy lost," Judge Hugo Francisco Alvarez, the judge presiding over the ceremony, told news reporters several weeks after the wedding. "He stared at the floor throughout the ceremony and when I pronounced him and Lisa Marie man and wife, he was reluctant to kiss her."

"There were no tears of happiness, no joy, no laughter. The ceremony had a somber tone. It was bizarre. I never heard him say he loved Lisa Marie Presley."

Now, I've been around long enough to know that this was nothing more than a publicity stunt. Michael had no desire for a woman. Not the natural desires that heterosexual men have, anyway.

What was unbelievable was that at about the same time this was breaking in the press, I received a call about another story that a newspaper was preparing to break. That story was that Joseph Jackson, Michael's father, had molested Michael when Michael was a little boy. So, while I put out denials about Michael's marriage to Lisa Marie, I also had to not only deny the Joseph Jackson story, but also do my best to ensure it didn't run. I succeeded.

However, when I informed the King about the stories, he appeared pleased by the denial of the wedding, but his reaction to the story about him and his father was strange, if not telling.

"How do you know that thing with Joseph never happened?" Those were the words from the King. I was stunned. Was he telling me that I should not have denied that story? Was he telling me that the story was true? He certainly acted in a manner that wouldn't confirm or deny.

It would make sense. I've heard psychologists and experts repeatedly state that most child molesters have themselves been victims of molestation.

So this news organization was onto something really big here. For if the king had been molested, it stood to reason that Michael Jackson too victimized others. But Joseph Jackson molesting Michael? Whoa!

LaToya Jackson claimed in her book and on television that Joseph had sexually violated her and raped her older sister Rebbie. Rebbie categorically denies that her father ever raped her. LaToya, nor anyone else, had ever so much as suggested that Joseph molested one of the boys.

Joseph's deviances in his marriage have been well chronicled, even having an affair that led to a child out of wedlock. But having spent a great deal of time around Joseph Jackson and knowing "The legend of the Hawk," I found this molesting charge hard to believe. And I was well aware that Michael Jackson often makes statements as a way of gaining sympathy or as a way to try to completely throw off a subject.

Still, the games Michael played with Lisa Marie were enough to drive anyone crazy and to cause any spouse to seek divorce. I remember talking to an attorney who informed me that the King had told him that Lisa Marie was jealous of the King's relationship with Princess Diana. My reaction was, of course, give me a break! The King didn't have a relationship with Princess Diana. He admired her, and a number of calls were put into Diana's people on behalf of Michael. He badly wanted to be friends with her, but apparently she wasn't the least bit interested.

Her people would always ask what the call was in reference to, and we'd have to leave messages saying simply that Michael wanted to speak with her. I personally made calls to the Princess and her assistant, a polite gentleman. I told him that Michael had matters he wished to discuss with the Princess. I was told to write down the subject matter in detail, send it along, and they'd get back to me. To my knowledge, none of those calls were ever returned.

The only time that I know Michael had an opportunity to meet face to face with the Princess was when he presented a hefty check to the Prince's Fund. At that time, both the Princess and Prince Charles were at the event to accept the check. Moments before taking the stage at a concert in London's Wembley Stadium, Michael proudly presented the Princess with a check for about $300,000 for the Prince's Trust, a charity for disadvantage children.

He also gave the Princess two tour jackets for her and Prince Charles. Author Christian Andersen said Michael was disappointed that the two young princes, William and Harry, who were six and three years old at the time, were not on hand. It was always this way with Michael. He thought so highly of himself and others just didn't see things that way. Later, he claimed to be a long time friend of Mohamed Al Fayed, even though while in London Michael would never visit them at their store, Harrods.

The King was troubled by his wife Lisa Marie's independence, as well as the situation that she had much more money than he did—a fact he never wanted her to know.

Whatever we did would always have to be the biggest and the most expensive. If we signed a contract for one million dollars, when it was reported to the press it had to be reported that the contract was for twenty million dollars, or that it was more than anyone else would be getting. Michael was adamant about such matters.

Every time Michael appeared on the Soul Train Awards, as part of the agreement to appear, we had to make sure that there were enough fans to create havoc. At the 1996 World Music Awards in Monaco, Michael wanted the producers to allow a fan to break through and run up to the stage and get to him, so that the world could see how intense his fans adore him.

However, the producer wouldn't allow that to happen. The security team stopped each and every effort for that to take place, much to the chagrin of the King.

When Michael appeared at the MTV Awards in 1995, I had to go to two or three local organizations in New York City to convince them to cart in kids to be outside when the King arrived at Radio City Music Hall for the awards.

The New York Press *got a hold of the way we were doing thing, ridiculing the King of Pop for it. Later we were really lambasted when Body Sculpt, who sponsored the Children's Choice Award and brought kids out to Radio City for his entrance, needed financial support and we didn't provide it.*

We had no money. We gave them a block of tickets for Michael's scheduled December show for HBO at New York's Beacon Theater. We told them to sell the tickets and they'd receive some of the proceeds from the sale.

It was around this time that Michael and Lisa Marie did their infamous interview with Diane Sawyer on ABC Television. Barbara Walters was very angry that she didn't get this interview.

She had made several direct calls to Gallin in an attempt to secure the interview, but they passed and went with Diane Sawyer.

All of the pre-programming prior to the appearance with Diane Sawyer was mired in chaos. It nearly became a mockery. We were all at the Sony studios. Johnnie Cochran, Howard Weitzman, Sandy Gallin, Jim Morey and myself. Lisa Marie and her staff were in a separate trailer.

During the breaks, when everyone could advise the King, since ABC wouldn't allow lawyers or anyone into the studio, we'd be prompting Michael on what to say. The attorneys were especially concerned because of the recent settlement with the 12-year-old Rent-a-Wreck boy. The producers of the show would not relent. They still would not allow the managers, Gallin and Morey, his attorneys or anyone else into the room where the show was being taped.

When the show was over, members of the legal staff and the managers met with the King to evaluate the appearance and how they felt it would be accepted by the American public. I have never been aware of any major involvement with the King that had not been pre-arranged, and like all others, this Diane Sawyer interview had been entirely arranged, planned out and thoroughly choreographed.

After the interview, the 12-year-old's uncle sued ABC for defamation of character He also said Michael violated the settlement's confidentiality agreement. The crux of his argument was that the network and Sawyer, desperate for ratings, gave the King a huge soapbox to tell the world that he was innocent of the child-molestation allegations. In the process, the Rent-a-Wreck Uncle also claimed, his brother—the accuser's father—was depicted as an extortionist who tried to shake down the King.

In the middle of all of this was Lisa Marie. The King was still trying to lead Lisa Marie into believing that he had as much, if not more, money than the value of the Elvis Presley estate. She had no idea of the mess she was getting into when she agreed to marry Michael Jackson.

But Lisa Marie had also unknowingly broken some rules. She had become attached to Jackson, which was a mistake. Worse though, she befriended his family, which had always been taboo. Lisa Marie Presley had driven to the family's Hayvenhurst estate in Encino, California and introduced herself to her in-laws.

Oh, Michael hated that. This was a no-no. He didn't want her associating with trash, which is what he thought of his own family.

Lisa Marie began confiding in Jackson's older sister Rebbie, who tried to ease Lisa Marie's troubles with Michael. Lisa also began forming a relationship with the Jackson's other superstar, Janet.

Meanwhile, Michael Jackson's "HIStory" CD fell off the charts just as fast as it hit. His career was seriously flagging.

He had been contracted to do an HBO special entitled "One Night Only." The network had promised a worldwide audience of 250 million people. But once again the King of Pop was up to his old tricks.

Something happened and he decided he didn't want to do the shows despite his agreement with HBO. You had to figure that he was up to something and he didn't disappoint.

I had attended the rehearsal for the show at the Beacon Theater earlier that day and all seemed to be going very well. However, later, after I left, I got a call from Jim Morey saying that I better get back there because they were taking Michael Jackson to the hospital in an ambulance. Morey said I needed to rush back in order to be available to the media.

Another sensational story lead-in: Pop star Michael Jackson was hospitalized today after collapsing during a rehearsal for an HBO concert special in New York.

The King had gotten his doctors to admit him after collapsing on stage. He was taken to Beth Israel Medical Center.

The block of tickets we had given to Body Sculpt for the children's charity were, of course, no good. So those kids from that organization that had been bussed in earlier for Michael's appearance received exactly nothing from the King.

At the hospital, he had a private second-floor room, which later became filled with his favorite characters. There were giant framed posters of Shirley Temple, Clark Gable, Mickey Mouse and Topo Gigio. Much to his delight, Diana Ross visited him. He allowed visits from his mother and Rebbie, but Bill Bray had to talk him into letting his wife, Lisa Marie, visit. Bill had to explain to Michael that the media would crucify him if he turned his own wife away.

Michael had a penchant for staging illness and other problems to get out of commitments and promises he had made. I remember being ordered to return from the Black Radio Exclusive Convention in New Orleans. Norma Staikos called and said Michael needed to meet with me. I was to meet him at his Wilshire condo, known as the hideaway.

What motivated all the drama? The King was concocting a hoax to get out of commitments he had made to Disney's Michael Eisner and Universal's David Geffen. He had promised that he'd attend the opening of their respective theme parks, but, as per usual, he reneged on the promises and needed an explanation.

Some of the details of what happened wound up in J. Randy Taraborrelli's book. Taraborrelli wrote that Jackson was negotiating with Disney Studios to lend his name in some way to a new robotic attraction. At the same time, David Geffen wanted Michael to appear at the opening of the Universal Theme Park in Florida, as did Steven Spielberg. Michael Eisner told Michael that if he had anything to do with MCA-Universal, Michael Jackson would never again be associated with Disney.

Michael could not bear the thought of being shunned by Disney. As a result of Eisner's dictate, he was torn. He desperately wanted Disney and Michael Eisner in his corner, but he also wished to maintain his friendship with David Geffen and Steven Spielberg. He anguished over this matter for weeks until the problem grew even bigger than it actually was.

Upon my return to California, I had to join the King and his doctor to discuss how we would fake an illness and have him admitted to St. John's Hospital in Santa Monica, California. At the appointed hour on the morning of June 3, 1990, his doctor would ring my phone and I would rush to the hospital. In the meantime, I had to arrange for someone to tip off the Associated Press to stimulate the media. I arranged for a lady friend of mine to call the Associated Press, offering to sell them information that she had seen Michael Jackson being rushed into the emergency room of St. John's Hospital. It worked like a charm.

We then had to issue daily reports on his condition, which fooled the media. However, many did question why his doctor, a plastic surgeon, was Michael's attending doctor during this stay.

Coincidently, a few days after he was hospitalized, Elizabeth Taylor checked into the same hospital for legitimate reasons. Reportedly suffering from pneumonia, Liz Taylor was put in a room right down the hall from Michael Jackson.

For days, Michael Jackson's hospitalization made the headlines he so often craves. The president, Liza Minnelli, Elton John and many others called to wish him well. He loved every bit of the attention.

David Geffen said that he always knew Michael was faking and wasn't experiencing any medical problems. Blanca, the King's former maid, has been quoted saying that Michael often pulled these hospital stunts just to see how many gifts and flowers he'd receive.

But Lisa Marie had had enough. While she seldom stayed at the ranch, since she and Michael mostly stayed at her home in the

San Fernando Valley, Lisa Marie wanted out of Neverland.

Lisa had hated it when Michael brought his nephews and little friends to her home. He would join them running around the house and creating havoc. They were out of control and she couldn't say a word.

Lisa seemed very genuine. I remember going to Memphis for a giant Elvis celebration on October 8, 1994 at the Pyramid in Memphis. Following the celebration, Lisa took us to Graceland. The place was filled with Elvis memorabilia and it had the same furniture as when the King of Rock and Roll had lived there.

Elvis is buried in a small garden behind Graceland and among the goings-on during Elvis Week are concerts, parties and a candlelight vigil where fans walk along a driveway to the gravesite. The Memphis tourism bureau estimates that tens of thousands of people visit the city during Elvis week each year.

The graveside procession, which grew from a spontaneous fan gathering the year after Elvis died, has been run by Elvis' estate since Graceland opened to the public in 1982. It is said that Graceland and its complex of shops and museums now draw nearly three quarters of a million visitors each year.

Unlike Michael, Lisa Marie was so down to earth. We met this black lady who essentially raised Lisa Marie. During our visit, she made us soul food, which Lisa Marie loved. The feast included fried chicken, macaroni and cheese, sweet potato pie, collard greens and more. Michael, of course, no longer eats this food.

During the Motown years when Michael was young, we'd hit all the popular barbecue and soul food joints. He certainly ate soul food when he was younger. But now the King of Pop didn't want to be connected to his black roots in any way, so he wouldn't indulge.

Who could be surprised by the news that Lisa Marie was through with the King of Pop? His own bragging words had made him look so silly. Remember, for the entire world to hear, he boast-

ed, "Just think, nobody thought it would last." Well, now it was over. Over. Over and out.

Barely 20 months after they married, Lisa Marie filed for divorce from Jackson, citing irreconcilable differences. Finally, this callous ploy, a mission to prop up Jackson's deteriorating public image, was over.

Lisa Marie had always been a tremendous supporter and believer of the King. However, it was rather strange that she married him and rarely stayed at the ranch.

More recently, I've heard rumors that Michael has attempted to call and talk with Lisa Marie. Supposedly, she hung up the phone after she realized he was stoned.

Michael had always been concerned with his legacy. I remember him reminding me that the most important thing to him was that legacy. So as part of my duties, I was to help create and maintain his legacy. He feared the fates of Nat King Cole, Sammy Davis Jr., and others who had tremendous talent but who Michael felt were forgotten after their deaths.

Michael desired to be remembered and worshiped like Elvis Presley. In preparation for his demise, Michael has saved all of his costumes and numerous Michael Jackson related merchandise. He wants to be bigger than Elvis when he finally meets His Maker.

Country music superstar Kenny Rogers, who knew Elvis Presley as well as Michael Jackson, said in a televised interview that "Michael is the Elvis of his generation. And, he too, is locking himself away from the real world. That's an extremely unhealthy way to live. I know what it's like to be mobbed by fans every time you go out. It can be terrifying. But, he's seen out so rarely that when he's spotted, it's a major event, and he gets mobbed. He's got to learn to get out more."

But the once-promising legacy of Michael Jackson has now been so badly tarnished it seems impossible to rescue. Expressing his deeply-felt fears to yet another, Michael told Ebony/Jet pub-

lisher John H. Johnson that he didn't want to end up like former Heavyweight Boxing Champion Joe Louis and others who made millions of dollars over their careers and then died broke and forgotten.

Publisher Johnson would often attend financial meetings on Michael Jackson's behalf, even flying in on his own dime to assist the King. Later, when Johnson had become very ill, I literally begged Michael Jackson to at least call the man. After all, Johnson had done so much for Michael. But I don't think the call was ever made. That is how unappreciative Michael Jackson is of those who have done for him.

Some, however, are very much tuned into Michael's many manipulations and refuse to put up with them. For example, Steven Spielberg had taken ill once and Michael decided to send a gift. He sent Spielberg a video camcorder, upon which the legendary director promptly marked "Return to sender." He didn't want anything from Michael Jackson.

Since the Rent-a-Wreck boy's accusation, Michael Jackson has been obsessed with how he is viewed in the media. That disastrous imbroglio severely damaged him, which was obvious by the lackluster sales of "HIStory." While the CD did debut at the top of the pop music charts, it quickly faded from memory.

Co-author Stacy Brown has said many times to Bob Jones, to Jackson family members and to others that the unbelievable success of "Thriller" had grown into a millstone around Jackson's neck.

It would be impossible for him to ever again attain that level of success. His many eccentricities—including the Elephant man's bones fiasco, his forever-changing looks and the farcical marriage to Lisa Marie—all haunted him.

Any attempt to create an at least somewhat respectable legacy was stymied by Michael's "HIStory" CD. Full of weird, messianic imagery, the double CD contained songs that sounded like the ravings of a crazed, confused and angered addict who'd been exposed.

One thing is certain. Michael will not be forgotten. But will he be remembered as a misunderstood and unfairly maligned legend, or a monstrous, self-hating, mentally ill deviant?

6

What's Love Got to Do with It?

"What's love but a second hand emotion?"

—Tina Turner

"Who could have imagined Michael Jackson would do something so...conventional? The Gloved One gave matrimony another chance Thursday and married the woman carrying his baby."

—The Associated Press, announcing Michael Jackson's marriage to Debbie Rowe, a nurse in his dermatologist's office

Within a year of his divorce to Lisa Marie Presley, Michael remarried. This time he wed Debbie Rowe, a nurse in Jackson's dermatologist's office. Of course it wasn't that Michael had found the love of his life. After all, what's love got to do with it?

At the time of the wedding, Rowe was already seven months into a pregnancy. Spreading like wildfire was the rumor that Rowe had been artificially inseminated as a favor to her friend, Michael Jackson.

This marriage almost didn't happen. Lisa Marie Presley actually had a thing for Michael Jackson and for a time she wanted him back. She not only would seek assistance from Michael's

95

family in trying reunite with Michael, but Lisa Marie also often called me and Johnnie Cochran asking for help in her quest to get back her husband.

Most of us thought it was a great idea for Michael and Lisa Marie to reunite. There was one problem: Debbie Rowe. Previously, Debbie had reportedly been pregnant for Michael, but she miscarried.

We, of course, knew that had Debbie's pregnancy been successful, Lisa Marie wouldn't have stood a chance. Any conciliatory efforts we could put forth would be in vain. Debbie quickly became inseminated again, and this pregnancy looked like a success. Lisa Marie Presley was out of the picture.

The marriage and the entire set up with Debbie Rowe was nothing more than a sham. Michael Jackson wasn't the least bit interested in Debbie Rowe. He was only interested in her churning out those blond-haired, blue-eyed babies."

It was twisted from the very beginning. Michael didn't want to have what he called "a splaboo," a black child. Anyone who believes those kids Debbie bore were his are as lost as Michael is out of touch.

Lisa Marie, when married to Michael, was said to be angered beyond words when Michael told her that Debbie Rowe offered to give Michael a child. This offer had been made shortly after Michael married Lisa Marie.

Apparently, Debbie Rowe's offer was a serious one, and it freaked out Lisa Marie. So it somehow was no surprise that immediately following the divorce to Lisa Marie, Debbie and Michael announced to the world that Debbie was pregnant with his child.

The couple's first child, Prince Michael, was born in February 1997 at Cedars Sinai Hospital in Los Angeles. Debbie Rowe barely got to see what her newborn son looked like, as Jackson almost immediately had the baby wrapped up and rushed to Neverland.

This happy family story grew even more surreal when Debbie admitted in an interview that Michael Jackson was raising Prince by his lonesome. Her excuse was that even if she did see the boy on a more regular basis, she'd have little to do because Michael pays so much attention to him.

Sure he does. He had a team of nannies and nurses looking after the child as he measured the air quality in his room every hour.

In 1998, Debbie Rowe gave Michael a little girl named Paris Katherine. This little girl was born at the Spaulding Pain Medical Center in Beverly Hills, a different hospital this time because the King had paid the bill at Cedar's very late after Prince was born.

On April 3, my office received a call from the television show "Extra," informing us that Paris Michael Katherine Jackson had been born that morning. They wanted confirmation from us on the baby's name and the place she was born since the situation at Cedars had became common knowledge.

"Access Hollywood" also called with the same information, but I still had nothing to say except "No comment." "Inside Edition" called around 3:30 p.m. with more specific information. On top of the story, they knew not only where the baby was born but also who had been the attending physician. Michael's secretary then asked me to confirm this information through my contacts at the hospital, no easy task given confidentiality agreements.

Evvy, Michael's assistant, wanted me to go to "Access Hollywood" and get them to reveal their sources to me. I refused.

The circumstances surrounding the birth of Michael's second child were even stranger than the first. Michael spoke of the events that occurred immediately following her birth: "I snatched her and went home with all the placenta and everything all over her. I'm not kidding. Got her in a towel and went home and washed her and everything was fine."

His own words wash clear any notion that Jackson resembles anything like an everyday guy. Snatching a baby and running home with the "placenta and everything all over her" is about as normal as, well, Michael Jackson.

Also there's the fact that an examination of the placenta can yield information that may be vital in the immediate and later management of both the mom and the baby. This examination can also yield information that may be essential for protecting the doctor in the event of an adverse maternal or fetal outcome. Although some medical experts, and Michael Jackson is no expert, argue that a pathologist should examine all placentas, most hospitals don't mandate this examination.

This fool just snatched the baby and ran with the placenta and everything ... He didn't want Debbie to form any kind of natural bond with the children, which is why he immediately snatched the babies and kept her from her children.

He paid off Debbie, buying the right to have it his way. A traditional marriage was not what Michael sought with any woman. What was really laughable were media reports suggesting that Michael married Debbie after she became pregnant in order to placate his disapproving mother.

Pluh-ease! *First, Katherine approved of nearly everything the King did, and even if she didn't Michael could care less. Katherine was nothing more than the person that had given birth to him. He had gone out of his way to adopt Elizabeth Taylor and others as his "mother."*

The real truth behind the marriage to Debbie Rowe was that Michael was doing a lot of business at the time with Saudi Prince Bin Talal Bin Abdulaziz Al Saud Alwaleed. They were forming a venture called Kingdom Entertainment to develop a variety of entertainment activities. The Prince had a worldwide string of Kingdom entities through which he had invested in banks, theme parks and other ventures. Michael Jackson was hoping to pursue such ventures as animation, theme parks, theme restaurants, television programming and motion pictures. Their first joint venture was Prince Alwaleed sponsorship of the "HIStory" world tour.

The Prince found out about unmarried Debbie's pregnancy and insisted that Michael and Debbie be married. It was common knowledge that Muslims believed that you must be married before you have children, so Michael flew Debbie over to Australia and married her. The gesture was really to please Prince Alwaleed. Because he had all the money, Michael was in no position to disappoint him.

When prosecutors called Debbie Rowe as a witness in the current case in April 2005, they were surprised by her testimony. Debbie, ever so loyal, expressed a desire to be reunited with Michael Jackson and her children, who she admitted she hasn't seen in 6 years.

The prosecution really miscalculated Debbie. She has always been a tremendous fan of Michael's and her desire is not only to see the children, but as she says, to be able to see Michael Jackson. She did a great job on the witness stand to ingratiate herself with Michael. Perhaps he'll now consider allowing her to visit with him and the children.

Many people believed that Debbie's testimony was so damaging to the prosecution that it was the deathblow to the entire case.

7

Enemies Be Damned

"Ye have heard, that it hath been said; thou shalt love thy neighbor, and hate thine enemy. But I say unto you, bless them that curse you, do good to them that hate you, and pray for them which despitefully use you, and persecute you."

—Matthew 5:43, 44 (King James' Version)

*A*lready knowing the truth, the reports didn't surprise me. The news stories were vivid too. Michael had attended a voodoo ritual in Switzerland where a witch doctor put a voodoo curse on David Geffen, Steven Spielberg, Jeffrey Katzenberg and several others on Michael Jackson's enemy list.

He paid $150,000 so that they would be cursed and hopefully killed, according to a lawsuit filed by Jackson's former business partner Myung Ho Lee. The ritual included bathing in a tub filled with animal blood. Lee was ordered to wire the money to a bank in Mali for a voodoo chief named Baba. It was said that forty-two cows were sacrificed for Michael's blood bath.

What was the point he was trying to make with these guys? The bottom line was simple: Geffen and company had long since tired of Michael Jackson's crap. They had moved on from dealing with him, which infuriated him. How dare anyone ignore the King? He was the high man on the totem pole, or so he thought.

Michael didn't care who he offended, much less cared whether he actually destroyed a person. Michael Jackson has always cared for just one person, that being himself. And as earlier related, he

101

had already tried to get Nation of Islam Minister Louis Farrakhan to publicly denounce these Jewish "friends" of his, but the minister refused to get involved.

He had written the song "They Don't Care About Us," which included those controversial lyrics, "Jew me/sue me/everybody do me." That song was made with a purpose and nobody can tell me differently. Everything Michael does has a purpose. He seeks attention and grabs it.

Tom Tugend of the Jewish Telegraphic Agency in Los Angeles perfectly captured the drama. He described how the blowup surrounding the Michael Jackson and the Jewish Question flared and heated a diplomatic storm, then ended just as quickly as it had begun.

Diane Sawyer had asked Michael Jackson about the staccato hip-hop song, in which Michael Jackson casts himself as the voice of universal victimhood. Michael was shocked at the suggestion that the lyrics ("kick me/kike me/don't you wrong or right me") might be considered anti-Semitic. "The song symbolized all victims of prejudice," he said. "It's not anti-Semitic because I'm not a racist. I could never be a racist. I love all races from Arabs to Jewish people."

Actually, Michael even hates his own real race, black people. He has zero cultural sensitivity and is completely out of touch. This brings to mind an interesting trip to Tel Aviv with Michael. In Jerusalem, he wanted to visit the famous Wailing Wall.

According to the Bible, Moses said Israel should have a single center of worship and for centuries that place was known as the Temple in Jerusalem. After its destruction, Jews continued to pray in the direction where it had once stood. Since the 16th century, if not earlier, they focused on a surviving section of its western retaining wall. Those who visited there often wept over the loss of the Temple, and it came to be known as the Wailing Wall.

Certain rules had to be followed, but Michael Jackson followed nobody's rules. He was to wear proper attire among other things. Do you think he did? No, he did not. He wore his usual regalia, a costume with the arm band, hat, etc.

Michael Jackson was a scandal in Israel and created a scene in Jerusalem. Israelis became incensed with him, as it was believed that he showed no respect for the sanctity of the wall.

And now the fact that Michael wrote this offensive song about "kick me/kike me/don't you black or white me" became a problem. He even had the audacity to mention Geffen, Spielberg and Katzenberg when defending the song. He said his three best friends were Jewish.

While Geffen seemed a bit forgiving of Jackson's words, Spielberg was considerably less forgiving. He was already upset that the booklet accompanying the "HIStory" album quoted him as calling Michael Jackson a phenom and one of the world's most precious resources. Spielberg said those statements were made earlier about a different album. He put out a statement saying those words were "no means an endorsement of any new songs that appear on what has now been released as Michael Jackson's HIStory album."

After that slap, Michael Jackson took a blood bath with a voodoo doctor to try and have Spielberg and company hexed. Now, can it get any weirder?

Michael's longtime desire to be in movies was well-known throughout the industry, and the Peter Pan theme has been woven into the fabric of Michael Jackson's image.

He cried his forever-fake tears to Jane Fonda when she told him that Peter Pan would be the perfect character for him to play.

What was ironic was that Steven Spielberg was working with others to produce and direct a Peter Pan movie. Would one of Michael's "best Jewish friends" come through for him and cast him in the lead role, as is his dream? Hell no.

With the role of Peter Pan out of the question, Jackson turned his attention to his music label's big film, "Men In Black." Michael wanted and eventually received a cameo role in the sequel to "Men In Black" because he mistakenly thought the film was a tear-jerker rather than a comedy.

> Michael had a meeting with the director of "Men in Black II" and told him that he had cried during the first film. The fact that this hadn't been that type of movie offers even more proof of how out of touch this guy is. Michael reached out to the higher-ups at Sony, trying to get them to put him in the sequel.
>
> Get this: he wanted to replace Will Smith. Yes, he told them to get Will Smith out of the movie and let Michael have his part. Kevin Mclin, who later did public relations for Michael, said Michael even offered to do the movie for free if they gave him Will Smith's role. This offer took place during a meeting with Amy Pascale, head of Tri-Star films and John Calley, head of Sony USA.

Will Smith is one of film's biggest box office draws, but the King tried to use his waning influence to get Will Smith tossed from the film. "No matter what it takes, I want to wear that black suit," Michael Jackson said of being in the film.

Jackson even made enemies of people trying to help him. Myung Ho Lee and his Union Finance and Investment Corporation would later sue Michael Jackson because Jackson didn't fulfill a number of promises he'd made to Lee, thus costing millions. In addition to giving Michael Jackson career advice, Lee had begun arranging loans and setting up investments. Referring to the King of Pop's finances, Lee later said in court papers that "Michael is a ticking financial time bomb waiting to explode at any moment."

Lee had arranged loans for Michael Jackson in the belief Michael would use this money to help secure the entire Sony/ATV (aka Beatles) catalogue. But Michael later told Lee that he had used the $140 million that Lee had secured for him to help settle his divorce from Debbie Rowe. Michael Jackson had also taken out loans of more than $200 million from Bank of America.

Michael got involved with Myung Ho Lee during some ill-fated concerts that were to take place in Seoul, South Korea. Obviously, the King failed to do his part so he became indebted to Lee. Because of this, Michael put Lee in charge of his business affairs.

Everything was catching up to the King. Unpaid bills were mounting and services were being cut. MLS Limousine cut off our company. We lost messenger service, as well as other credit lines. And Myung Ho Lee was only one of a long list of others who'd embarrass the King with lawsuits.

Concert promoter Marcel Avram was asked to pay a substantial amount of money Michael Jackson owed doctors back in Germany.

Word had it that it was so very important that these doctors be paid because they had illegally prescribed painkillers for Michael Jackson.

Michael Jackson had admitted in 1993 that he had checked himself into a rehab for an addiction to painkillers. Avram handled concert tours for Jackson in 1992, 1993, 1996 and 1997, and thought he was about to do another when the King of Pop reneged.

Avram agreed to pay the German doctors because Michael had agreed to hire Avram as the promoter on his next world tour. When Avram heard that the King had been flapping his gums to others about a new tour, it drew his ire. He had sent many letters to Michael that had gone unanswered.

Michael was scheduled to do two Millennium concerts, which were planned for Sydney and Honolulu. Just as I figured he would, Michael backed out of these shows, which apparently cost Avram a lot of money.

Avram sued, seeking more than $25 million in damages. Eventually, he won the case. A jury in Santa Maria awarded him nearly all of the $5.9 million in lost profits he sought.

Michael spent several days testifying in the case, during which he again made worldwide headlines. What drew everyone's attention this time were photographs featuring Michael's bandaged nose. Suddenly, everyone could see the disastrous effects of numerous plastic surgeries.

Still unwilling still to admit defeat in this case, Michael Jackson's attorney Zia Modabber spun it saying that it was in some respects a victory for Michael because Avram had originally sought more than $25 million.

That's the Michael Jackson I have come to know all too well. He was never willing to acknowledge that he'd done anything wrong or that he'd been beaten in any way. His pride and his ego were as large as any as I had ever encountered in all my years in Hollywood.

If you were an enemy or even perceived as an enemy of Michael Jackson's you were a marked man. Sometimes you didn't even have to be enemies to be marked. Michael had once enjoyed a cozy relationship with Paul McCartney. On several occasions, the McCartney's had invited Michael to their home in Europe. And, after all, Paul McCartney was really the discoverer of Neverland.

Author J. Randy Taraborelli told the story of McCartney entertaining Michael at his home in Europe while the duo was recording a song. One evening after dinner, Paul McCartney displayed a thick booklet of song titles to which he owned the rights. He told Michael that this was how to really make the big bucks: publishing.

Michael Jackson was intrigued. He owned the publishing rights to his own songs. Obtaining those rights were one of the reasons he and his brothers left Motown and Berry Gordy's

Jobete publishing house. Still, before this moment, Michael had thought of publishing as a tedious business, one primarily concerned with collecting royalties and licensing material for other media.

Paul McCartney explained how lucrative publishing could be, especially thanks to the CD explosion and the increased use of popular songs in advertisements, movies, and television.

Taraborrelli said that, as it happened, Paul McCartney and John Lennon had sold their copyrights to a publisher named Dick James when they were young. James ended up making a fortune on the Beatles' songs. Then in the late sixties, while The Beatles were on vacation in Rishikesh with the Maharishi Mahesh Yogi, for tax reasons James sold Northern Songs—the company that continued to hold the rights to the Beatles' compositions. Purchasing it was Sir Lew Grade's ATV Music, Limited.

ATV was later purchased by Australian businessman Robert Holmes a Court's Bell Group. With ATV, McCartney and Lennon's estate split the songwriting revenue generated by 251 of their songs written between 1964 and 1971, including "Yesterday," "Help," "A Hard Day's Night," "The Long Winding Road," "Hey Jude," and "Let It Be." ATV also held the publishing rights to thousands of other compositions, including songs by The Pointer Sisters, Pat Benatar, and Little Richard. For the next couple of hours, Paul and Michael discussed publishing, and Michael absorbed everything. Taraborelli said Paul McCartney would regret the conversation.

After that visit, Michael and Paul remained somewhat friendly, but Michael now kept his distance. He didn't want Paul to perceive him as being anything more than an acquaintance, perhaps because he had a plan.

"Michael's the kind of guy who picks brains," Paul McCartney said in an ABC Television interview. "When we worked together, I don't even think he'd had the cosmetic surgery. I've got photos of him and me at our house, and he looks quite different. He's had a lot of facial surgery since then. He actually told me he was going to a religious retreat and I believed him. But he came out of that religious retreat with a new nose. The power of prayer, I guess."

Charles Koppleman was part of a group that outbid the more than the $47.5 million Michael Jackson later bid for the Beatles' catalogue. However, Koppleman's bid was rescinded after his backers bailed at the 11th hour and Michael became owner of this valuable property.

The irony: It is expected that Koppleman, who had been recently charged with the responsibility of helping Michael Jackson maintain the catalogue, will soon outright own Michael's share of ATV.

8

Hall of Shame

"Everyone has a past. Even Hollywood stars and performers. And nine times out of ten, the lives of these present day stars and icons are quite different than how we know them. We have accepted this, but we just don't understand it."

—Fadetoblack.com

The culmination of any artist's career arrives when a legacy has been established. For a musician, this legacy may be cemented with a nomination and election into the Rock and Roll Hall of Fame. Once elected, one of the most anticipated moments for fans and artists alike is the now famous jam session held at the Rock and Roll Hall of Fame's induction ceremonies. It seems that every living artist desires to strut his or her collective stuffs at the end of the ceremony in the jam session.

Once again, Michael Jackson has proven that he's not like any other artist and that his desires are quite different. For one, mingling with peons has never been a favored activity of Michael Jackson's.

Faking a broken leg had to suffice. Michael appeared at the 2001 Rock and Roll Hall of Fame ceremonies walking on crutches with a cast covering one of his legs.

As usual, this was a ploy. The King didn't want to have to answer to critics or anyone else about his choosing not to perform or even to hang around to watch other honorees perform.

One of the many rumors flying around that night at New York's Waldorf Astoria Hotel, where the ceremony had been held, was that the King had been too high to perform.

'N SYNC had inducted him, which was fitting: handsome, young white boys honoring him. What could be more appropriate in the eyes of Michael Jackson?

But the rumor was afoot that Michael Jackson was on drugs, that he had been much too high to do anything. What a shame.

Whatever reason, he just didn't perform. It could also be that he'd realized that if he did, he'd be the only one there lip-synching.

Michael once lip-synched an entire show on the "HIStory" tour so that he could get through the show. So lip-synching wasn't at all unusual for the King of Pop.

The 1995 MTV Awards performance was lip-synching. But, lip-synching at the Hall of Fame? Nah, even he had to know this was unacceptable. It would mean the end of all relevance in music for the King of Pop.

The end was indeed approaching for the King of Pop. Following his Hall of Fame induction ceremony, Michael Jackson met with producer David Gest to begin laying the groundwork for a tribute concert to himself.

It was to take place at Madison Square Garden in New York City on September 8 and September 10, 2001. The concerts would be billed as a 30th anniversary celebration of Michael Jackson in show business. It would be timed to coincide with the release of his new CD "Invincible."

A lot was riding on this CD. Sony Music had sunk $30 million into Michael Jackson's budget for the record. They were hoping to move about twenty million copies. With a CBS special and a concert tour, they could potentially sell a lot of records. Michael Jackson could rightfully continue his King of Pop prominence and all would be well again in Jacksonville. It should be noted too that Sony had no advance knowledge of the September anniversary concerts, since Jackson and Gest effectively shut them out.

The concerts featured a slew of special guests: Elizabeth Taylor, of course; Liza Minnelli; Whitney Houston; N'SYNC; Britney Spears; Luther Vandross; Ray Charles; Marc Anthony; Destiny's Child; Shaggy; Gloria Gaynor, and Chris Tucker, as well as a reunion of The Jackson Five.

> *This was purely a money move on Michael Jackson's part. The last thing in the world he wanted was to perform with his brothers. He had made it clear to all who worked with and for him that his family was to be kept as far away as possible. He was determined to stay away from those people. This is a man whose dressing room was off limits to his own parents.*
>
> *He would only have little boys in his dressing room. He'd have games for them to play and other things designed to keep his little friends occupied. Nobody was allowed and family was strictly not allowed.*

While the two concerts sold out, they hardly created the buzz Jackson and Sony had been hoping for. The significance of the two evenings was totally lost only hours later when America was attacked on the ill-fated morning of September 11.

As airplanes flew into the World Trade Center, the Pentagon, and crashed outside of Pittsburgh, in New York Michael Jackson scrambled to find friends Elizabeth Taylor and Marlon Brando. It was also reported that Jackson also sought a place of refuge "underground."

Despite his aging parents and his siblings also being in New York (as well as the fact that he has nieces and nephews who make their home in Manhattan), Jackson's concerns were solely for Taylor and Brando.

He made this clear in an interview with *Vibe* magazine. He told the magazine how he was in New York and had gotten a call from friends in Saudi Arabia that America was being attacked, and he screamed down the hotel hallway to all of his staff.

Michael told *Vibe* that he yelled for everybody to get out, to leave now! Marlon Brando was on one end of the hotel, his security was on the other end, and Elizabeth Taylor was at another hotel.

Michael told how they jumped in the car, but there were these little girls who had been at the show the night before and they were banging on the windows, running down the street screaming. Fans are so loyal. He then said how he and Liz and Brando hid in New Jersey.

Meanwhile, Jackson's family had to depend on sister Janet Jackson to rent Winnebagos to carry the clan across the country and back to California. Jermaine and Katherine Jackson called co-author Stacy Brown from their hotel room the morning of September 11, frantically asking how to get out of Manhattan and to the borough of Queens, where Janet had reserved them Winnebagos.

Says Brown, "They expressed a fear of going over any bridges or through any tunnels, which is the only way to get to Queens from Manhattan. After instructing them, they again phoned me and asked for directions from Queens to New Jersey and, eventually, across the country. They also asked whether I had heard anything about how Michael Jackson was doing."

With numerous big name artists lining up to perform tribute songs and shows, Michael sought to join them. It was not to be. As journalist Clay Risen wrote, "It couldn't have happened to a freakier guy. The King of Pop is a pop star pariah. Michael Jackson's invitation to sing on a September 11 tribute album was turned down by a platoon of big name stars."

Michael Jackson produced his own charity song. Although Michael contended that the song ("What More Can I Give?")

was written for September 11, it had been previously recorded by Jackson for a benefit concert featuring Luciano Pavarotti some years earlier.

Michael Jackson doesn't give freely. That's been a misapprehension for years. But this was what led to his hooking up with porn producer Mark Schaffel. Schaffel arrived on the scene just at the moment when the guy usually responsible for Michael's filmwork wasn't being paid.

Then the media got wind of Schaffel's scandalous background and a firestorm of controversy was unleashed. It was reported that Michael Jackson had approached McDonald's restaurant about funding a video for victims of the September 11 attacks. However, when Schaffel's background came to light, McDonald's pulled out of consideration.

I was told that the lawyers took Michael Jackson in a room and starting playing pornographic material and said to him that this is what Schaffel does. They told him to get rid of Schaffel. But the King does what he wants to do and kept Schaffel around.

According to a report in the *Los Angeles Times*, Schaffel met Jackson through Beverly Hills dermatologist Arnold Klein and they became friends. The *Times* also reported that when Jackson found out about Schaffel's past career, his managers begged Sony to kill "What More Can I Give?"—fearing it might revive controversy surrounding Michael Jackson's settlement with the family.

For his part, Schaffel told newspaper reporters that his porn background helped speed along the project with Michael Jackson. He said the project was done very quickly and very cheaply, "the way things are done in the adult film business. We didn't waste money the way they do in the music business. Why shouldn't this charity single come out? Because of something I did in the past? I mean, this is an industry in which rock stars date porno queens. Adult film doesn't have the same stigma it used to. So really, what's their excuse?"

Not long after the September 11 attacks and the Mark Schaffel fiasco, Jackson encountered more personal problems: his alleged drug abuse had come to the fore. His family had become concerned and they planned an intervention in New York in December. *The National Enquirer,* as usual, had the story:

> A bizarre-acting Michael Jackson is hooked on drugs and booze and his frightened family flew across the country to save his life.— The Enquirer reported.
>
> *People often say that the stories reported in the* Enquirer *and* Star *are just fabricated gossip. Well, that is just not the case. Over the years, so-called insiders and even family members themselves sold stories to the Enquirer. Michael Jackson even sold pictures to the tabloids.*

The report on Michael's drug usage said a stubborn Michael flatly refused his family's pleas to get treatment. He banned his family from staging any other emergency interventions. *The Enquirer* quoted a source as saying that Michael's family feared for his life. They believed he was out of control on drugs and alcohol.

Janet, Rebbie, Tito and Randy flew on a chartered jet from Los Angeles to New York to confront Michael Jackson. They had received frantic calls from a senior member of Michael Jackson's staff saying he was walking around like a zombie. The staff member said Michael was hooked on Demerol and was drinking large amounts of wine.

To make matters even more alarming, it wasn't the first time. The tabloids had reported in 1999 that Michael was hooked to an intravenous drip that sent doses of a prescription painkiller surging into his veins.

They reported that Michael had been seen taking large doses of Demerol, which has potential side effects including disorientation, hallucinations and mental sluggishness. Michael Jackson had first admitted being hooked on painkillers in 1993, while under duress from child molestation allegations.

Dr. Steven Hoefflin called the MJJ office to check on Michael, telling me that something needed to be done since Michael Jackson was out of control and listening to absolutely nobody. Dr. Hoefflin said if action wasn't taken soon, he expected Michael to commit suicide or, at the very least overdose.

Dr. Hoefflin said he had spoken with Michael's attorney John Branca just before calling me, and that he was going to insist that Branca try and set up a meeting with Michael and have all of the people who have known him for a longtime to be at the meeting and to help try to save his life.

9

Financial History

"Stop pressuring me, stop pressuring me."

—Michael Jackson, the 1995 song "Scream"

With all of the trouble Michael Jackson has seen, it's no wonder that the erstwhile King of Pop is teetering on the brink of personal insolvency, his creditors now unwilling to extend new loans.

> *The reports have been everywhere. Michael is facing an immediate monetary crisis. I know that the important due date on his $70 million Bank of America loan has come.*
>
> *His business managers Charles Koppelman and Al Malnik are desperately trying to deal with the situation, but seems inevitable that he's going to lose everything.*

At least two groups of financial investors have backed out of deals with Michael Jackson, scared off by the molestation allegations. At this point, his finances are, well, just about HIStory.

Jackson's most valuable asset is the Beatles catalogue he owns jointly with Sony Music as part of the ATV Music Publishing. It has an estimated value of nearly $1 billion.

On top of the $70 million loan with Bank of America, there is another $200 million loan guaranteed by the ATV music catalogue and he is also leveraged for an additional $250 million to buy other music libraries.

Look, when you spend $2 million a month, you run into these problems. This guy has been unable to face the fact that he no longer brings in income to support his spending habits.

Buying expensive gifts for Elizabeth Taylor, Marlon Brando, Liza Minnelli and other famous so-called friends, along with the millions he's had to pay these boys, their attorneys, his attorneys and others—all of this has caught up with him.

As I previously mentioned, the MJJ offices were closed and we had to work out of our homes because Michael could no longer pay the bills. The messengers weren't being paid, the limos, hospitals, and there were some reports that some payroll checks weren't clearing.

Hamid, the guy who shot video for Michael Jackson, was owed tens of thousands of dollars. I mention him because he had been so extremely loyal and for that he was now getting screwed.

I also understand that Jonathan Exley, Michael Jackson's personal photographer is owed about $200,000. Having received instead just a check for $10,000, he was understandably upset too.

Rumors persist that Michael Jackson sought a refinancing deal. Just imagine that. This from the guy responsible for "Thriller," the bestselling album in history. Michael Jackson made more than $100 million alone off that album, but his very expensive lifestyle and various legal problems has left him with a cash flow problem.

In 1995, when Michael Jackson's ATV Music Publishing Company merged with Sony Music Publishing, Michael was said to be worth $1 billion. *Newsweek* claimed that back in 1998 Jackson was about to sign a bond deal and over two years later, the *London Sunday Mail* reported he was trying to raise $350 million by issuing bonds backed by the copyrights of his own songs and those of the Beatles.

In January 2002 Jackson turned to Sony for a loan, borrowing $200 million from them against the Beatles catalogue. Sony also gave him $30 million to finance the making of Invincible. Speculation spread that he would file for bankruptcy.

Michael Jackson's apparent desperation manifested itself in a very public way when he attacked then-Sony music chief Tommy Mottola, calling him a racist and "very, very devilish." At a press conference in New York City, Michael Jackson was named the first member of a coalition formed by the controversial Reverend Al Sharpton and Johnnie Cochran to investigate whether record companies are financially exploiting artists.

Still once again, Michael was using somebody, and this time it was Al Sharpton. It never ends with Michael Jackson. It's absolutely ridiculous for him to claim that he was being financially exploited by Sony.

Michael Jackson said record companies have to start treating their artists with respect, honor and financial justice. He went on to address comments from unnamed Sony executives, who had said that Jackson owed the company $200 million for studio time and promotion. Michael said that was outrageous and offensive.

Of course, Sony issued its own statement saying they had never issued any statements, verbally or in writing, claiming that Michael Jackson owes them $200 million. They claimed to be baffled by the comments.
We were all baffled!

The feud with Sony was featured on several Web sites, which were set up by fans who said that the label had stopped promoting "Invincible." The flames were further fanned when music mogul Russell Simmons and singer Ricky Martin sided with Sony Music's Tommy Mottola in the feud.

Jackson's brother Jermaine got into the act with a press release of his own. Jermaine Jackson asked Stacy Brown to write the release and the following was what Stacy Brown issued on behalf of Jackson:

"The financial records related to the $55 million Sony Music claims it has spent making and promoting "Invincible" are inflated and far from accurate. We believe that the amount of record sales attributed to Michael Jackson is underestimated.

There are numerous artists who are deceived by record companies who overwhelm them with lawyers, accountants, publicists, double talk, false practices and shady business dealings.

It is important that my family continue to stand behind Michael during these tumultuous times.

When he is being attacked, every one of us is being attacked. Furthermore, my brother is black and no one has the right to question his race as he has done so much for so many of all races.

We believe that Tommy Mottola has used nepotism and cronyism to assure total financial control.

We want a complete listing of each person involved in every aspect. Russell Simmons and Ricky Martin are uninformed and should wait to hear the facts before making derisive statements about Michael.

The people that Michael has working for him should stand up for him. When he faced child molestation allegations in 1993 they didn't stand up for him.

His family was left to take the fight to the media to refute the terrible allegations against him. I hope that Michael now understands that he must rid himself of those who only want to reap the benefits of being associated with him yet does nothing for the good of him.

It is also our intention to insure those gifts of petty handouts, past or present, do not compromise all those who support Michael and our family.

We want to assure all that together we can fight racism in the music business without limitation.

We demand that Sony Music sign a full disclosure clause agreeing to justify each and every artist's account, record sales, distribution cost, and publicity accounts.

Furthermore, we want Sony to disclose standardized payments to artists similar to professional basketball contracts and we call on all negotiations to be regulated by draft placement and set by a minimum and maximum salary.

Michael's talents are God-given and neither Tommy Mottola nor anyone else can take it away from him. He has earned his place in popular music history."

The fact that Jermaine Jackson's statement was largely ignored was no surprise. Jermaine had a burning desire to please Michael and did whatever he could to draw public attention to his defense of Michael.

According to Jermaine's secretary Lawanda Lane, most in the music industry had absolutely no respect for Jermaine. All refused to comment on his statement.

Michael Jackson did little to promote "Invincible." Though he performed two high-profile concerts in New York and held a CD signing in Times Square, he did not tour. He also granted almost no interviews.

Sharpton teaming with Jackson was almost comical. Sharpton told everyone afterwards that he didn't know that Jackson would carry on the way he did by calling Mottola a racist. The civil rights activist and presidential candidate said his initiative is willing to work with the Record Artists Coalition, a similar artists rights group that was formed with Sheryl Crow, Don Henley and others.

Sharpton told the *New York Post* that he had known Tommy Mottola for fifteen or twenty years, and "never once have I known Tommy Mottola to say or do anything that would be considered racist. I was taken aback and surprised by Michael Jackson's remarks."

Michael Jackson had further escalated the conflict by holding up posters of Mottola with horns and called him devilish. Jackson also claimed Mottola had described another black artist with a racial slur.

Jermaine Jackson later identified the artist as Irv Gotti. "He called Irv Gotti a fat black nigger," Jermaine said.

But the brothers' ally Sharpton said the Jacksons had gone too far in slamming Mottola. Sharpton said Mottola had always been supportive of the black music industry. Further, Sharpton added, Mottola was the first record executive to step up and offer to help blacks with respect to corporate accountability.

Russell Simmons, the founder of Def Jam Records, said Michael Jackson was simply upset that his "Invincible" CD didn't sell. Simmons said that fact had nothing to do with Sony or Mottola.

"There are two things I know," Simmons told reporters including Stacy Brown. "Tommy Mottola is not a racist, and, in black music, you don't need $30 million to make an album successful. Michael Jackson's album didn't sell because Sony failed to promote it; it failed because of a lack of quality. If a record is a hit, it'll sell on its own."

Even former Michael Jackson manager Frank DiLeo chimed in against the singer. "Tommy Mottola is not a racist," DiLeo told Stacy Brown. "This whole thing about Michael looking to put the blame for a bad record on somebody besides himself, and it's an unfortunate way to do it. Despite what Michael Jackson says, he has been making his own marketing and management decisions for twelve years now. What that kid really needs to do is to stand in front of a full-length mirror and take a good hard look at the real problem."

DiLeo spoke from experience. As Jackson's manager, DiLeo had guided Michael through the most success any artist had ever achieved, but had been fired in 1990 largely—it is believed—because DiLeo was said to have taken too much credit for the Jackson phenomenon.

The press reported that Michael had fired DiLeo because DiLeo had bungled a major multimillion deal for the domestic theatrical release of Michael's ninety-minute video "Moonwalker."

The project had cost Michael approximately $27 million, according to biographer J. Randy Taraborrelli. "Moonwalker" was theatrically released in Japan, but not in the United States because of numerous disagreements.

It was reported that DiLeo was behind the decision not to release "Moonwalker" in the United States, which angered international distributors who had bought the film for theatrical releases. When the announcement was made that there would be no domestic deal, many overseas theaters pulled the film, or scaled down promotion and publicity. This cost Michael millions in lost box office revenue in the United States and abroad.

In the end, DiLeo came up with a multimillion-dollar offer to distribute the film domestically, and someone else in Michael's camp talked Michael out of it. So while Michael may have been angry at the way the distribution of the film was handled, he wasn't angry enough at that time to fire DiLeo.

Another issue with Frank DiLeo was that Michael had become disgusted with his tabloid image, one that he believed DiLeo was continuing to propagate. But the truth was that it was Michael, not Frank DiLeo, who planted these stories in the tabloids.

What doomed DiLeo was Michael's overwhelming and obsessive desire to have his "Bad" album top "Thriller" in sales. Even though Frank DiLeo's guarantee of producing five straight # 1 singles from the "Bad" album was realized, Michael became unbelievably jealous of the attention and acclaim DiLeo was receiving.

Are you kidding me? Michael Jackson is the King. The be-all-to-end-all. Nobody was supposed to receive attention, be commended, and much less lauded, but the King himself.

Michael Jackson had his attorney John Branca call Frank DiLeo to tell him his services were no longer required.

DiLeo went on to accomplish something that Jackson still dreams of: landing roles in big time movies. DiLeo acted alongside Robert DeNiro and Joe Pesci in the Mob hit movie, "Goodfellas."

10

The Devil Himself

"He is the devil himself. He's not a good man. He's evil."

—The mother of Michael Jackson's latest accuser

"He is the devil in God's clothes."

—Raymond, the uncle of 1993 Rent-a-Wreck accuser

"The devil keeps transforming himself into an angel of light."

—The Bible

The writing had been on the wall for a good long time now. I had long known this day was coming. I had warned Michael about his interactions with these little white boys. After the Rent a-Wreck boy, one would have hoped that he'd learned a hard and valuable lesson.

It was all too creepy for anyone to defend and put a good public relations spin on it. The young boy in the current case had been there. The newspapers had published the facts about the creepy lair that they described as Michael Jackson's dark secret room, perched behind a trapdoor at Neverland. This, according to media reports about the testimony the boy and his brother will give at trial, is where he'd take the boys to commit lewd acts.

The chamber, concealed so well that police who twice have scoured the place in recent months may have missed it. No one—not outsiders anyway—knew about the door hidden behind clothes at the back of a walk-in closet in Michael Jackson's bedroom. The closet that hides the secret entrance is packed with military-style costumes, children's toys, and books.

Beyond the door is a narrow carpeted stairwell lined with rag dolls descending into a secret chamber.

It is a twisted version of a young child's bedroom. A bed is adorned with pillow cases imprinted with Peter Pan's face and the word "Neverland." Sitting on the bed is a redheaded, bug-eyed stuffed doll, and on a nightstand next to the bed is a Mickey Mouse telephone. On the wall are pictures of smiling diapered babies.

Whatever may have happened to these boys probably happened here. This bizarre room appears to be the haven of a twisted individual, a mad genius. I ask myself, what is loving and caring and warm about this dark and secret room?

After the Rent-a-Wreck family case was settled, we were told that Michael Jackson was being watched closely. There was much talk about the statute of limitations, things of that nature. Say what you will about whether these people, the young boys and their parents, are doing this for money, the fact is that Michael Jackson has brought this trouble onto himself.

Again and again, I tried to tell him to be careful with these little boys, that the press was going to eat him alive parading around with these boys.

And now the King of Pop is on trial. His life is in the hands of a jury, a judge, prosecutors and lawyers. It has come to that point.

I've been inundated with calls and questions from the media since this case began and especially since my firing in June of 2004. People want to know what I saw. They ask why I didn't speak up. They want me to tell them absolutely whether Michael's guilty or not.

What did I see? I saw a mad genius in Michael Jackson. Someone who toyed with people, someone who loved and cared only for himself. I saw a master of self-promotion and a self-destructive multi-millionaire spending millions trying to buy friendships and favors, whether it was from little boys or Louis Farrakhan, Princess Diana or Elizabeth Taylor.

I saw a man who embarrassed himself at Katharine Hepburn's house. Katharine Hepburn had thrown a dinner party in Michael Jackson's honor. He had arranged to have his photographer wait outside her house.

During the party, he asked to speak with her privately. She obliged, and that's when he asked if he could take a photo with her. She said absolutely not. He then proceeded to tell her how he'd seen all of her movies, but when she quizzed Michael on his favorites, he was unable to name any.

While I was suspicious, I never had any concrete evidence that Michael was actually engaging in criminal activity. Yes, I'd knew boys would stay with him in his hotel suite. And I had witnessed the strangely affectionate holding of the hands and the petting of the hair. But don't forget this is the weirdest man on the planet. I never witnessed molestation.

Going to the authorities was not an option. There was nothing to report. Should I go and say, hey police officer my boss is walking around holding hands with little boys? Hell, Michael Jackson went on worldwide television and said there was nothing wrong with that. It was no secret. You must understand too, that I was called to testify in the Grand Jury proceedings in 1993 and didn't duck my responsibility. I certainly wouldn't lie.

Michael Jackson also knows I wouldn't lie. His father's attorney, a weird woman by the name of Debra Opri, stated that I am a disgruntled ex-employee with an axe to grind. That's the camp's battle cry: someone has an axe to grind. I don't have an axe to grind; I simply felt I had a story to tell.

Debra Opri had reached out to me to get to Michael Jackson. As soon as this case broke, Debra reached out to someone in the James Brown camp to get close to Michael Jackson It was MJJ Productions who gave her Katherine Jackson's assistant's phone number. So I was the one who got her in, and now she says I'm a disgruntled ex-employee. Everybody knows she is working for the Jacksons free of charge.

Michael Jackson's brother sent a messenger to fire my secretary and me. After working for and with Michael Jackson for thirty years, not only did he allow me to be let go in such a low-class fashion, he even refused to pay any for my unused vacation. I didn't even receive a courtesy phone call.

Some have suggested that I should consider it to have been an honor to work for Michael Jackson. That thought is absurd. Why write a book? This is what some have asked. When you're constantly asked to tell your story and defend your own actions, there comes a point when you want to set the record straight. Now is that time for me.

Is Michael Jackson guilty of child molestation? I'll leave it to a jury to decide that question. They are the ones charged with that responsibility. Nevertheless, I have witnessed some of the oddest behavior in a superstar that one could imagine.

But again, I repeat: I did not witness sex between Michael Jackson and any of these little boys. I can't say whether or not it happened. I can only offer you an opinion. Perhaps in reading this book you'll be able to discern what that opinion is.

To quote the *National Enquirer*, "Today Michael Jackson stands a ruined man. He and public relations pros like Bob Jones have made many attempts to mend his image but have all failed. Mostly, Michael Jackson has failed. He is no longer perceived as sweet and shy, sensitive and talented. He is no longer seen as the little boy who charmed the world but as the man-child who interferes with little boys."

During testimony in a civil court in Santa Barbara, California in November of 2002, the *New York Daily News* and *New York Post* photographed Michael Jackson up close. Both papers ran cover photos of him and both reported that a photo of him taken earlier that week showed that his nose was disintegrating.

The *Daily News* article focused on what they called Michael's excessive and abusive overuse of plastic surgery. The paper ran a series of six photographs taken previous to the recent photograph snapped at the courthouse. They showed the progression in Michael's looks from 1972 through 1998 as he altered himself through plastic surgery. He went, of course, from being a really handsome African-American kid to an awful facsimile of a Caucasian woman.

ABC News joined others in doing an exposé of Michael Jackson's nose. In a February 2003 special, the network reported that although Michael Jackson said in a new documentary that he has had only two operations on his nose, a leading plastic surgeon believes he has had so much work done that he is now a "nasal cripple."

Dr. Pamela Lipkin, a prominent New York City plastic surgeon studied photographs taken of Jackson at a California court appearance in November—in which his apparently scarred nose was covered by a small transparent bandage.

She believes something went terribly wrong. "What I think happened recently is that something in his nose—a graft, an implant, something—has now come out through the skin," Lipkin told ABC.

Although Jackson's face has been splashed across the tabloids in recent months, Brittan Stone, photo editor at the celebrity magazine *Us,* says the singer's face is not being seen on magazines. "The one thing you can't do with Michael is a beauty shot, because that shot simply just doesn't exist any-more," Stone said. "I don't think you can put Michael Jackson's face on the full-page of a magazine. ... I think the flaws in his face become a little too evident, a little too frightening. It becomes like a medical study."

In the Bashir documentary, Michael Jackson said the only surgery he had had on his face were two operations on his nose to help him breathe more easily and so he could hit higher notes. He denied having any surgery done on his lips, cheeks, chin or eyes.

After reviewing photographs taken at different points of Jackson's career, Dr. Pamela Lipkin offered her opinion. The first photograph showed Jackson with the Jackson Five in the early 1970s. "At that point, Michael Jackson's [a] very normal, very cute, Afro-American child, with actually very good fea-tures. You know: good lips, high cheekbones, and good bone structure. Even skin tone, I might add," Lipkin said.

In a picture taken with Diana Ross at a publicity event for the musical movie "The Wiz" in 1977, Jackson, who was then 19, looked similar to his childhood photos, but in a picture taken with Ross at an awards show four years later, his face was "starting to get a little bit more interesting," according to Lipkin. "Obviously he's had some nasal surgery," she said. "The width of the nostrils is dramatically reduced. ... The bridge is much thinner. ... And you know something, that's a great result. Having started with that nose, that nose is still believable."

Three years later, by the time Jackson's next album, Bad, hit it big in stores, his appearance had evolved again. By this point, there were rumors that he was undergoing plastic surgery to change the shape of his face. Lipkin believes photographs from the time show evidence of more procedures. "His eyebrows are very, very high, so he's probably had some sort of forehead lift, or brow lift," she said. "His eyes, I'm not sure. He probably did have some fat removed around his eyes. They're particularly naked-looking."

Lipkin also said Jackson's lips appeared to have been thinned out, and noted that a cleft had appeared in his chin that was not there before. "That's not a natural cleft," she said. "You can tell." She said she knew of a technique for creating a cleft chin, but that it was not popular because "it never looks real."

By 1991, when Jackson's song "Black and White" was a huge international hit, people began to wonder whether he was lightening his skin. On the song, he sang, "I'm not gonna spend my life being a color." In 1993, Jackson told Oprah Winfrey that his skin color was indeed changing—because of a skin disorder called vitiligo which causes white blotches to appear on the face and other parts of the body. "It is something that I cannot help, okay?" he said on Winfrey's show. "But when people make up stories that I don't want to be who I am, it hurts me."

When studying a photograph of Jackson taken at the time, Lipkin's initial reaction was to call it "the most unusual case of vitiligo I've ever seen." Although she said it was possible that Jackson started bleaching his skin because of the disease—in order to blend his natural darker tone with the lighter blotches that were appearing—she also said that a lighter skin seemed consistent with other changes that she believes Jackson made to his features. "When you look at the other features, the skin bleaching sort of goes along with what I think was his quest for beauty," she said. "So I have to wonder what came first? Vitiligo or lighter skin?"

In 1995, at the age of 36, Jackson released "HIStory." In the video for the song "Childhood," his appearance was strangely wide-eyed, square-jawed, narrow-cheeked, and his skin was like porcelain. "Probably he's trying to look Caucasian," was Lipkin's reaction. "His skin is whiter. His nose is getting thinner every six months. His lips are getting thinner. His eyebrows are getting higher. His eyes are getting wider every time. His cheekbones are getting bigger."

In a 1999 interview, Dr. Stephen Hoefflin, a plastic surgeon who operated on Jackson's nose, said he did not believe the singer was trying to appear less African-American. "I think he wanted a feature that bothered him to be made smaller, more sculptured. And certainly not to erase the ethnicity." Hoefflin added that Jackson had undergone more surgery than he recommended.

In the Bashir documentary, Jackson said that when he was growing up his father used to tease him about the size of his nose, but he rejected any suggestion that he was trying to change his appearance or to appear more white. "I don't control puberty and I don't control the fact that I have vitiligo," he said. He said his face had "squared out" in adolescence, and that he had never done anything to change it. "I have had no plastic surgery on my face—just my nose," he said.*

*Reprinted, by permission, from "Surgeon: Michael Jackson a 'Nasal Cripple'", ABC News Online February 8, 2005

SUPERIOR COURT OF THE STATE OF CALIFORNIA

FOR THE COUNTY OF SANTA BARBARA

SANTA MARIA DIVISION

THE PEOPLE OF THE STATE OF CALIFORNIA,	)	No. 1133603
Plaintiff,	)	**INDICTMENT**
v.	)	Count 1 — Violation of Penal Code § 182
MICHAEL JOE JACKSON,	)	Counts 2-5 — Violation of Penal Code § 288(a)
Defendant.	)	Count 6 — Violation of Penal Code §§ 664/288(a)
	)	Counts 7-10 Violation of Penal Code § 222

COUNT ONE

The Grand Jury of the County of Santa Barbara, State of California, by this

Indictment, hereby accuses MICHAEL JOE JACKSON of a felony, to wit: a violation of Penal

Code section 182, subdivision (a)(1) (CONSPIRACY), in that on or about and between

February 1, 2003 and March 31, 2003, in the County of Santa Barbara, State of California, he

did conspire with

                                                                    and other uncharged co-

conspirators and co-conspirators whose identities are unknown, to commit the crimes of:

1

Found   Not Found

✓   ___   a violation of Penal Code Section 278 (CHILD ABDUCTION), a

felony;

Found   Not Found

✓   ___   a violation of Penal Code Section 236 (FALSE IMPRISONMENT), a

felony;

Found   Not Found

✓   ___   a violation of Penal Code section 518 (EXTORTION), a felony

and that pursuant to and for the purpose of carrying out the objectives and purposes of the

aforesaid conspiracy, to wit:

did commit one or more of the following overt acts in the State of California, at least one

of them in the County of Santa Barbara:

OVERT ACT NUMBER 1 [THROUGH OVERT ACT NUMBER 28]

2

INDICTMENT

COUNT TWO

The Grand Jury of the County of Santa Barbara, State of California, by this Indictment, hereby accuses MICHAEL JOE JACKSON of a felony, to wit: a violation of Penal Code section 288, subdivision (a) (LEWD ACT UPON A CHILD), in that on or about and between February 20, 2003 and March 12, 2003, in the County of Santa Barbara, State of California, he did willfully, unlawfully, and lewdly commit a lewd and lascivious act upon and with the body and certain parts and members thereof of John Doe, a child under the age of fourteen years, with the intent of arousing, appealing to, and gratifying the lust, passions, and sexual desires of the said defendant and the said child.

The further allegation that in the circumstances of the crime alleged in this count the crime constituted substantial sexual conduct with a child under the age of fourteen years, within the meaning of Penal Code section 1203.066, subdivision (a)(8) is

Found   Not Found

COUNT THREE

The Grand Jury of the County of Santa Barbara, State of California, by this Indictment, hereby accuses MICHAEL JOE JACKSON of a felony, to wit: a violation of Penal Code section 288, subdivision (a) (LEWD ACT UPON A CHILD), in that on or about and between February 20, 2003 and March 12, 2003, in the County of Santa Barbara, State of California, he did willfully, unlawfully, and lewdly commit a lewd and lascivious act upon and with the body and certain parts and members thereof of John Doe, a child under the age of fourteen years (the second molestation concerning which John Doe testified), with the intent of arousing, appealing to, and gratifying the lust, passions, and sexual desires of the said defendant and the said child.

The further allegation that in the circumstances of the crime alleged in this count the crime constituted substantial sexual conduct with a child under the age of fourteen years, within the meaning of Penal Code section 1203.066, subdivision (a)(8) is

9

INDICTMENT

1 Found   Not Found

2   ✓   —

3

4   **COUNT FOUR**

5   The Grand Jury of the County of Santa Barbara, State of California, by this

6 Indictment, hereby accuses MICHAEL JOE JACKSON of a felony, to wit: a violation of Penal

7 Code section 288, subdivision (a) (LEWD ACT UPON A CHILD), in that on or about and

8 between February 20, 2003 and March 12, 2003 in the County of Santa Barbara, State of

9 California (in the first molestation witnessed by James Doe), he did willfully, unlawfully, and

10 lewdly commit a lewd and lascivious act upon and with the body and certain parts and

11 members thereof of John Doe, a child under the age of fourteen years, with the intent of

12 arousing, appealing to, and gratifying the lust, passions, and sexual desires of the said

13 defendant and the said child.

14   The further allegation that in the circumstances of the crime alleged in this count the

15 crime constituted substantial sexual conduct with a child under the age of fourteen years,

16 within the meaning of Penal Code section 1203.066, subdivision (a)(8) is

17 Found   Not Found

18   ✓   —

19

20   **COUNT FIVE**

21   The Grand Jury of the County of Santa Barbara, State of California, by this

22 Indictment, hereby accuses MICHAEL JOE JACKSON of a felony, to wit: a violation of Penal

23 Code section 288, subdivision (a) (LEWD ACT UPON A CHILD), in that on or about and

24 between February 20, 2003 and March 12, 2003, in the County of Santa Barbara, State of

25 California (in the second molestation witnessed by James Doe), he did willfully, unlawfully,

26 and lewdly commit a lewd and lascivious act upon and with the body and certain parts and

27 members thereof of John Doe, a child under the age of fourteen years, with the intent of

28 arousing, appealing to, and gratifying the lust, passions, and sexual desires of the said

                          10

1   defendant and the said child.

2   The further allegation that in the circumstances of the crime alleged in this count the

3   crime constituted substantial sexual conduct with a child under the age of fourteen years,

4   within the meaning of Penal Code section 1203.066, subdivision (a)(8) is

5   Found   Not Found

6

7

8   **COUNT SIX**

9   The Grand Jury of the County of Santa Barbara, State of California, by this

10 Indictment, hereby accuses MICHAEL JOE JACKSON of a felony, to wit: a violation of

11 California Penal Code sections 664 and 288, subdivision (a) (ATTEMPT TO COMMIT A

12 LEWD ACT UPON A CHILD), in that on or about and between February 20, 2003 and March

13 12, 2003, in the County of Santa Barbara, State of California, he did willfully, unlawfully, and

14 lewdly attempt to have John Doe, a child under fourteen years, commit a lewd and lascivious

15 act upon and with Defendant MICHAEL JOE JACKSON'S body and certain parts and

16 members thereof, with the intent of arousing, appealing to, and gratifying the lust, passions,

17 and sexual desires of the said defendant and the said child.

18

19   **COUNT SEVEN**

20   The Grand Jury of the County of Santa Barbara County, State of California, by this

21 Indictment, hereby accuses MICHAEL JOE JACKSON of a felony, to wit: a violation of Penal

22 Code section 222 (ADMINISTERING AN INTOXICATING AGENT TO ASSIST IN

23 COMMISSION OF A FELONY), in that on or about and between February 20, 2003 and

24 March 12, 2003, in the County of Santa Barbara, State of California, he did unlawfully

25 administer to John Doe an intoxicating agent, to wit: alcohol, with the intent thereby to enable

26 and assist himself to commit a felony, to wit: CHILD MOLESTATION, in violation of Penal

27 Code section 288, subdivision (a).

28 ////

                                        11

COUNT EIGHT

The Grand Jury of the County of Santa Barbara, State of California, by this Indictment, hereby accuses MICHAEL JOE JACKSON of a felony, to wit: a violation of Penal Code section 222 (ADMINISTERING AN INTOXICATING AGENT TO ASSIST IN COMMISSION OF A FELONY), in that on or about and between February 20, 2003 and March 12, 2003, in the County of Santa Barbara, State of California, he did unlawfully administer to John Doe an intoxicating agent, to wit: alcohol, with the intent thereby to enable and assist himself to commit a felony, to wit: CHILD MOLESTATION, in violation of Penal Code section 288, subdivision (a).

COUNT NINE

The Grand Jury of the County of Santa Barbara, State of California, by this Indictment, hereby accuses MICHAEL JOE JACKSON of a felony, to wit: a violation of Penal Code section 222 (ADMINISTERING AN INTOXICATING AGENT TO ASSIST IN COMMISSION OF A FELONY), in that on or about and between February 20, 2003 and March 12, 2003, in the County of Santa Barbara, State of California, he did unlawfully administer to John Doe an intoxicating agent, to wit: alcohol, with the intent thereby to enable and assist himself to commit a felony, to wit: CHILD MOLESTATION, in violation of Penal Code section 288, subdivision (a).

COUNT TEN

The Grand Jury of the County of Santa Barbara, State of California, by this Indictment, hereby accuses MICHAEL JOE JACKSON of a felony, to wit: a violation of Penal Code section 222 (ADMINISTERING AN INTOXICATING AGENT TO ASSIST IN COMMISSION OF A FELONY), in that on or about and between February 20, 2003 and March 12, 2003, in the County of Santa Barbara, State of California, he did unlawfully administer to John Doe an intoxicating agent, to wit: alcohol, with the intent thereby to enable and assist himself to commit a felony, to wit: CHILD MOLESTATION, in violation of Penal

INDICTMENT

1 Code section 288, subdivision (a).

2

3 ## SENTENCING ALLEGATIONS

4 It is further alleged that Counts Two through Five are serious felonies within the

5 meaning of Penal Code section 1197.7, subdivision (c)(6).

6 As to Counts Two through Five, it is further alleged pursuant to Penal Code section

7 1203.066, subdivision (a)(8) that the victim in the above offense, John Doe, was under the age

8 of 14 years and MICHAEL JOE JACKSON had substantial sexual conduct with John Doe.

9

10 NOTICE TO DEFENDANT: Conviction of the offenses alleged in Counts Two

11 through Five will require you to register pursuant to Penal Code section 290. Willful failure to

12 register is a crime.

13

14 NOTICE: Pursuant to the provisions of Penal Code section 293.5 the use of the

15 pseudonym "John Doe," as it appears in the Indictment, is for the purposes of protecting the

16 privacy of the alleged victim.

17

18 THOMAS W. SNEDDON, JR., District Attorney
   Santa Barbara County

19

20 By: _____

21 RONALD J. ZONEN (State Bar No. 85094)
   Senior Deputy District Attorney

22

23 By: _____

24 GORDON AUCHINCLOSS (State Bar No. 150251)
   Senior Deputy District Attorney

25

26

27

28

13

Epilogue

*I*t was very important for me to note that during all my years with Michael Jackson, he was the most famous person of African-American heritage in memory.

Over the course of my career, I worked with Louis Jordan, Jimmy Lunceford, Johnny Mathis, Sidney Poitier, Cassius Clay, Dinah Washington and many others. Given the huge talent of Michael Jackson, he was someone that all African-Americans could have been very proud of. In reality, he was bigger than Elvis Presley. Elvis was huge in the United States, but never performed around the world to the tens of thousands that adored Michael Jackson.

Michael Jackson lived in fear that he would one day be forgotten. However, by ignoring the advice of so many people, he destroyed himself, and the legacy that he so fiercely wanted.

I don't know that his quest to separate himself from black people was a contributing factor, but I do know that we as a people are the most forgiving in the world. After being ignored and abused by you, we still accept you back with open arms. Michael Jackson, though, now joins O.J. Simpson and a few others who had their honorary white membership rescinded when they stepped out of line.

Michael Jackson wasn't really looked at as a black man. He was the world's leading entertainer, but only in the United States of America will they always remind you that you are black if you step out of line.

Michael Jackson attempted to start a Holy War between the Jews and Arabs while he was with Prince Alwaleed and it didn't work. Michael Jackson didn't realize that to be one of the world's

richest men, Alwaleed must deal with all types. He's a business-
man. He's not foolish.

Michael Jackson had the opportunity to be a role model for all
minorities, but he chose to be one of the most disgraced perform-
ers ever to hit the stage because of his antics.

It was the British tabloids that first ran with the nickname
"Wacko Jacko" for Michael. They detailed his desire to buy the
Elephant Man's bones and how Michael wanted to buy Marilyn
Monroe's bones and display them at Neverland.

The tabloids reported that Michael had paid $1 million to
develop a potion that would make him invisible so that he and
his famous chimp Bubbles could go out to a shopping mall and
have a great time without people staring at them. There were
reports that Michael had placed in his will that Bubbles would
get $2 million upon Michael's death.

I hated that monkey, Bubbles. I never wanted it around me.

For nearly thirty years, Michael Jackson has been an icon.
He was the most celebrated popular music performer ever. He
had eclipsed Elvis Presley and the Beatles and was adored by
the masses. He proclaimed himself as Peter Pan and named his
ranch Neverland.

Now his Neverland estate is viewed as a sinister playground
designed to lure innocent children into his realm. He is the
punch line to scores of jokes by late night comedians and those
in the African-American community.

Michael Jackson has also become the focus of studies by
schools of higher education and a source of discussion among
researchers. In fact, Kimberley Jane Wilson of the National
Center for Public Policy Research wrote about various reactions
to Michael Jackson she'd come to notice.

There seem to be only two main schools of thought concerning the one-time "King of Pop," he's either guilty of

molesting a young boy and ought to be tried, convicted and put in a cell deep under a prison, or he's innocent.

Our criminal justice system has historically been indifferent or downright hostile to the fates of black men. Kimberley Jane Wilson said on her website that when she was five years old, she watched two beefy white police officers beat a black teenager to unconsciousness. One officer had literally held up the profusely bleeding kid while the other officer whacked him with his baton.

But Kimberley Jane Wilson points out that as hideous as those crimes against blacks were, it doesn't have much to do with Michael Jackson's predicament today.

There are those, activist Dick Gregory and comedian Steve Harvey among them, who believe that Michael Jackson was set up. They feel that the powers-that-be in the white community hate seeing a successful black person and every now and again, one or two must be taken down as a warning to the rest of the black community. Michael Jackson's wealth and power, so their reasoning goes, is too much of an affront.

First, although Michael Jackson is still wealthy by average guy standards, he's lost a shocking amount of money over the years. It costs a small fortune each year just to maintain his 2,700-acre Neverland estate's house, train, zoo and amusement park rides. *Forbes* magazine says Michael Jackson is worth about $350 million. *The New York Times* pointed out that his debts over-reach his worth. Compared to billionaires like Robert Johnson and Oprah Winfrey, Michael Jackson's financial mess doesn't look enviable at all.

Next, Michael Jackson's artistic influence is now nonexistent. Today, young people lean toward Beyonce, Usher, 50 Cent and others. Unless he somehow pulls together an astonishing comeback, Michael Jackson's years of musical genius are far behind him.

So many, like Kimberley Jane Wilson, say they are not buy-ing that there is a conspiracy to take Michael Jackson down, despite Jermaine Jackson's claim that Michael Jackson's November 1993 arrest was "a modern day lynching." Someone, Jane Wilson says, ought to send Jermaine Jackson a copy of Mamie Till Mobley's book "Death of Innocence and One Hundred Years of Lynching." Michael Jackson is not Emmit Till. He's not even Rodney King.

Most people feel that Michael Jackson's current legal trou-bles have nothing to do with race. Michael Jackson's own actions have simply caught up with him. Michael Jackson's repeated on-camera insistence that there's nothing wrong with having unrelated kids in his bed and his apparent fascination with boys makes him look worse than any slander invented by a malicious individual.

For Bob Jones, it really doesn't matter much anymore. After all, he is no longer charged with the gargantuan job of trying to resurrect Michael Jackson's career.

I don't know how anyone would go about doing that even if he is acquitted. It's a task that the best of Hollywood's public relations people couldn't successfully handle. It's really an impos-sible feat.

"Entertainment Tonight," "Access Hollywood" and "Extra" are camped out at the court house, as are Fox News, CNN, MSNBC, Court TV and Telemundo. E! airs daily re-enactments. CBS, NBC and ABC, and mainstream print outlets such as *The New York Times* are represented, alongside celebrity mags such as *People* and *Us Weekly*. Other media have come from Great Britain, Germany, Asia and Australia.

Yet as the trial progresses, editors and producers are divided over whether Jackson will remain water-cooler talk as Simpson and Peterson were. Although some say Michael Jackson's celebrity status warrants the extensive coverage, others say the subject matter—child molestation—will dampen interest as the case drags on.

CNN chief Jon Klein said on air that he doesn't want a repeat of the Simpson trial, which CNN was accused of milking for ratings. "The bar will be to not blend in with the background noise surrounding the case. If we've got something unique that takes us beyond the headlines, we'll do it," he stated, a sentiment seconded by Fox and MSNBC.

At the other end of the spectrum is producer Linda Bell Blue, who has dispatched "a small army" of 35 staffers from "Entertainment Tonight" and "The Insider" to Santa Maria to chart every twist and turn in the trial. ET has even rented a rooftop from a building across from the courthouse to get good camera angles. "There is worldwide interest," Blue told *USA Today*, and even if jury selection is fairly dry, there's always an eccentric Michael Jackson to watch entering and leaving the courthouse. "You never know what to expect when Michael Jackson walks into a courtroom with his family."

That said, some people predict that interest will fade because the trial won't be televised. And the judge has imposed a gag order on the principals, limiting the spin that marked the Simpson case.

Others also note that Jackson's star peaked in America fifteen years ago and that some minds were made up about him eleven years ago when he paid the Rent-a-Wreck Family boy more that $20 million to avoid a similar trial. "There are not that many people who can identify with Michael Jackson. You don't look at him and say, ''That could be a member of my family," says Bonnie Fuller, editorial director of American Media, which publishes *Star* magazine. "He has been a train wreck for so long. The fascination has abated." *Us* magazine editor Janice Min has a reporter covering Jackson but says, "The story is a major downer."

Rival morning shows NBC's "Today" and ABC's "Good Morning America"—which covered the Simpson and Peterson cases extensively—are staffed to handle every angle of this one. NBC has spared no expense, erecting a two-story scaffold platform outside the courthouse dubbed "Peacock Tower." But there still remains debate within those organizations over how much time over the long run they will devote to the trial. "The subject matter is a tough one," "Today" producer Tom Touchet said. "We have parents watching with their kids."

Cynthia McFadden, ABC's senior legal correspondent who made headlines by reporting secret grand jury testimony in the Jackson case, says ABC will cover the case aggressively. "While this is a story with some salacious aspects, it does not mean it's not important. These are extraordinarily serious charges, and a man could go to prison for a very long time if convicted of them."

While writing this book, my collaborator, Stacy Brown, and I have both been questioned by investigators in the Santa Barbara Sheriff's Department and the District Attorney's office. The questionings came after intense media interests in this project.

There was an assumption, taken on also by the Jackson family that we were going to "spill the beans," as it were. They were livid that two "loyal" individuals would write about Michael Jackson. That's why, as a pre-emptive strike, Joseph Jackson's attorney Debra Opri appeared on Fox Television and said "Bob Jones is a disgruntled ex-employee."

This statement came without any knowledge of what I was writing. Her words were ill-conceived and erroneous—typical of the Jacksons.

In their minds, it was supposed to have been an honor just to have worked for Michael and, for Stacy, just to be associated with them for so many years.

I've provided thirty years of service and Stacy has been a friend to the family for years as well. He has also witnessed many things firsthand and has heard things from their own mouths that they'd be horrified to have repeated.

Stacy has kept these things secret. What's more, Jermaine Jackson approached Stacy Brown three years ago to write a book about Jermaine and the Jacksons. This idea, however, drew the ire of Michael Jackson.

Other family members have, in the past, also approached Stacy about writing a book, so it is hypocritical of the Jacksons to blast this book, especially since they wanted Stacy Brown to do the same for them. Neither Stacy nor I owe the Jacksons the loyalty we've shown them.

It is true that my termination is a sore spot, but I'm aware that many people are terminated daily. Still, after thirty years with this man, I know that most people would have been furious by the shabby method of its execution.

If Michael Jackson is guilty of child molestation or any other crimes, it is difficult not to wonder what his parents and siblings were thinking about Michael's actions all these years. With the exception of his oldest sister, Rebbie, who wasn't around as much, and perhaps one or two other siblings, I don't see how they could not have known. Latoya claimed in her book that everyone else knew what Michael was doing. And Katherine frequently complained about the little boys around Michael.

These people have proven to be a different breed. The wacky tabloid reports that most of us have heard and, at least partly dismissed over the years have only scratched the surface of their weird and wacky ways.

Recently, in a faxed letter to his family, Randy Jackson told his relatives that the world views them as royalty. There was indeed a time when the Jacksons were compared to the Kennedys as America's royalty. That time seem like eons ago now as the actions of the family, particularly Michael, has successfully destroyed what once appeared to be an untouchable legacy.

The scandals, pitfalls and other embarrassments were mostly self-inflicted. Certainly the charges Michael Jackson now faces cannot be excused as some vendetta the prosecutor has against him nor as an act of racism.

Michael Jackson admittedly has paid millions upon millions of dollars because of accusations of improper conduct with minor boys. After the 1993 public scandal, anyone with a speck of common sense would not have continued publicly behaving with little boys the way he has.

In his youth, Michael Jackson brought an incredible amount of happiness to millions of people the world over. That is what those currently defending him remember most—not the forty-six-year-old disaster he's become. America's past and Michael Jackson's past are so strongly imprinted on many people's minds, they are blinded from seeing anything else.

AFTERWORD

The Current Case

In January 2005, the website The Smoking Gun offered the world a first glimpse of the People of the State of California vs. Michael Joseph Jackson. The charges were as hideous as anyone could have imagined, trumping many people's worst fears.

According to the government's case, which The Smoking Gun reported first, if the distressing allegations in these documents are true, Jackson is a textbook pedophile: a 46-year-old predator who plied children with wine, vodka, tequila, Jim Beam whiskey, and Bacardi rum.

The team prosecuting Jackson has relied heavily on the testimony of a teenage boy, his younger brother, older sister, and the children's mother. (At the time of the alleged incident, the victim, a cancer survivor, was thirteen, his brother was twelve, and their sister was sixteen.) In the documents, the brothers provide corroborating accounts of Jackson's alleged criminal acts. Together, they offered the Santa Barbara Sheriff's Department and District Attorney Thomas Sneddon a double dose of startling misconduct.

Their sister was never invited into the singer's bedroom, nor did she witness any sleazy behavior. However, she said in her deposition that the entertainer gave her and her brothers wine at Neverland and that both her siblings told her about dirty talk from Jackson. She said her older brother recounted Jackson providing tequila and Skyy vodka. Not surprisingly, he also wanted them to keep the drinking a secret from their parents. (As reported in *Vanity Fair*, Jackson often disguised wine drinking by having the alcohol put in soda cans. He then called it "Jesus juice.") The sister also related her older brother's discomfort when Jackson touched his behind through his clothes.

In the alleged conspiracy to imprison her family at Neverland, the accuser's mother has been the key witness for the prosecution. She contends that Jackson and several business associates began illegally scheming to keep her family caged up at Neverland the day after Martin Bashir's sensational documentary "Living with Michael Jackson" aired in the United Kingdom .

Though Jackson is the only person charged in connection with this purported plot, the performer's heavily redacted April 2004 indictment refers to five of his business associates. It indicates that aides Frank Tyson and Vincent Amen, business managers Dieter Wiesner and Ronald Konitzer, and video producer Marc Schaffel are accused of helping Jackson orchestrate this scheme, which included shipping off the family for safekeeping to Brazil. Family members were repeatedly told by the Jackson camp that the foreign move was necessary because numerous death threats had been directed at the family, according to investigative records cited in the indictment.

In a bid to buttress the conspiracy claim, prosecutors elicited grand jury testimony from several Jackson associates, most of whom dealt with the family post-Bashir. Those witnesses included Neverland employees like security chief Jesus Salas, guards Christopher Carter and Brian Barron, public relations aide Ann Gabriel, and Schaffel cohort Christian Robinson, who testified with limited "use immunity" about the filming of the family's so-called rebuttal statement, a videotape they told detectives they were strong-armed into making.

Naturally, the accuser's mother has been the chief target of the Jackson defense team, which has tried to portray her as a scheming grifter who has made up the accounts of abuse, feeding her children these sleazy stories. They contend she's after a big fat settlement. However, testimony from several witnesses, including comedian George Lopez, say the mother is not a grifter, but is simply a woman who has been abused and who only wants what's best for her family. In his testimony, Comedy Club owner Jamie Masada said that the accuser's mother has turned down money offers, instead asking for "just friendship and prayers."

The accusers' timeline just doesn't make sense, say Jackson's defenders. Following their proffered scenario, say Jackson's attorneys, the alleged conspiracy to silence the family began more than two weeks before the first molestation incident is alleged to have occurred. So the cover-up began before any crimes actually occurred? they ask.

Using information gathered in support of their court request to raid Neverland, the office of private eye Bradley Miller (a detective working for Jackson attorney Mark Geragos), as well as the L.A. home where Jackson's accusers filmed their rebuttal videotape, investigators drafted a long, very precise affidavit.

These papers deem Jackson's "three-year long interest" in the accusing boy "grossly abnormal" and, in itself, corroborative of the family's accusations. Detective Paul Zelis said investigators had established "reasonable probable cause" to "believe Michael Joe Jackson is a pedophile and one with the means to inhibit disclosure of his offenses by bribery and intimidation."

The brothers recounted to investigators two unsettling incidents, although neither boy could say exactly during which visit these events occurred. The younger brother said that while he and his brother were riding in a golf cart with Jackson, the King of Pop inquired, "What's your favorite curse word?"

He also recollects being in Jackson's bedroom along with his brother, Tyson, Jackson, and the performer's son. Tyson, the younger boy told investigators, connected his brother's laptop to the Internet, "and Michael started searching for pornographic web sites," according to Detective Zelis. The child said Jackson typed in either www.pussy.com or www.teenpussy.com and he and his brother saw photos of "naked ladies." The boy "described seeing a female holding her shirt up and exposing her breasts and Michael commented, 'Got Milk?'" The boy said that Jackson's son was sleeping nearby and the entertainer "told Prince he was 'missing out.'"

The older brother offered a similar account, adding that Michael told him not to tell his parents about these activities. When the younger boy told his sister about the porno photos, his older brother then "told her not to say anything because Michael would get mad. [He] told her everything is secret and that they can't say anything," according to Detective Zelis.

The sister was left out of most Neverland activities and days would go by without her seeing her brothers or Jackson She slept with her parents in a separate guesthouse while her brothers bunked in Jackson's bedroom. (Supposedly, the boys slept on the bed while Jackson and Tyson were in sleeping bags on the floor.)

The younger boy was also sometimes left out of Jackson's plans. His older brother said in one interview that Jackson wanted just him to stay the night in his bedroom, but he insisted that his brother be allowed to stay as well.

A letter from a girl named Renia located during the Neverland raid established girls as undesirables. A search warrant released later noted that the missive "discusses boys sleeping with subject. She was not allowed into 'Apple Head Club' because she was a girl."

That description of evidence item #361 was one of more than forty entries wholly or partially redacted from a Neverland search warrant inventory released last year. Santa Barbara Police Investigators, including Sgt. Steve Robel, have testified that the raid on Michael Jackson's bedroom suite turned up a cache of adult material, including photos of nude women and boys.

Listed in the inventory of material found in the police raid of Jackson's sprawling ranch were a photo of the child in his nightstand, a folder of e-mails about the youngster, and several letters and cards from the boy, who signed one letter with his charming nickname from Michael, "Doo Doo Head."

Supporting the Neverland raid was an affidavit listing what investigators were searching for, including magazines depicting lewd acts involving minors and/or adults, any photo of a minor without clothes, and any images showing and representing children and/or animals engaging in sexual conduct. Upon their surprise arrival at the ranch, they found plenty. There were four "Barely Legal" DVDs and the hustler documentary "Pimp Up, Ho's Down" Also seized were sexually explicit magazines like "Club," "Barely Legal," and "Couples"—found in a leather bag next to the bathroom sink, in a box at the base of Jackson's bed, in a Samsonite briefcase, and inside the nightstand. Seized item #365 is described as "2 books of photographs of nude women and boys, located in master bedroom."

The accuser had told investigators that, after sexual encounters, Jackson had him swap his dirty underwear for clean garments, so they kept their eyes open for the boy's brand and size. Included in the items found is #327, "Underwear: Hanes: White boys underwear located in Paris' bathroom." Paris Jackson is the singer's six-year-old daughter.

During the police raid, the officers cut off and took parts of Jackson's mattress, as well as his mattress pad. Found in Jackson's bathroom were open bottles of Jack Daniels and Pinot Noir, a book "containing nude photographs of men," two nude art magazines, and three "books containing nude photos in plastic bag."

Also seized were a "book containing pictures of children on beach," a photo inscribed "To Apple Head," a letter addressed "Dear Apple Head," commercially produced photographs of semi-nude girl, and a Liza Minnelli Christmas invitation.

The last time the older boy saw Jackson was when he spent time with the King of Pop and his children at Hollywood's Hilton Hotel around Christmas 2000. They watched a movie, the boy told investigators while lying in bed. They "talked, hung out, and wrestled around."

While Michael did not give any of the boy's siblings presents, according to the child's mother, Jackson gave the older boy a Nintendo or PlayStation unit and video games that Christmas. The next year they kept in touch by phone, speaking for hours at a time. There were no visits that following year, however, the child was undergoing chemotherapy for cancer and was too ill. In 2001, the accuser's mother complained to Michael about the lengthy telephone chats with her son. Jackson didn't take kindly to the criticism.

In her recollections of those calls, she told investigators that some things her son mentioned seemed "peculiar" to her. For instance, Jackson's favorite color was the same as her son's favorite color. And "whatever [her son] liked, Michael liked as well." She felt Jackson was having too much influence over her son. And soon after Michael found out her son was sharing details of their phone calls with her, the boy stopped related specifics about the chats.

These "endless phone conversations" and other "extravagant attention" paid to the boy by Jackson are, investigators, say, strangely similar to the account heard by authorities ten years ago by the Rent-a-Wreck kid. Of course that criminal investigation ended when the boy's family pocketed a $20 million civil settlement and declined further cooperation.

Evidence gathered in that earlier investigation has been introduced in Michael's latest trial. A detailed recounting of the criminal probe of Jackson was released to the media in 2004. The Rent-A-Wreck boy told police that Jackson frequently masturbated him, offering a detailed description of the star's penis as a way of proving the pair had been intimate. According to an affidavit, Rent-a-Wreck Family told police that Jackson justified the illicit acts by saying, "it was okay and natural because other friends had done this" with him. The singer, then in his mid-thirties, also allegedly told the boy that, "masturbation is a wonderful thing." The celebrity told Rent-a-Wreck boy that if he ever spoke about the sexual incidents, he would be "placed in Juvenile Hall," and they both would get in trouble.

According to the document, there was a confrontation between Jackson and Rent-a-Wreck Family's father Evan, who suspected that the performer might have been assaulting his son during sleepovers. The father found Jackson in his "hideaway apartment" in Los Angeles, then asked, "Are you fucking my kid?"

Michael answered that he did not use that word. Linden notes that the singer did not answer the question or deny the allegation. The earlier Rent-a-Wreck Family investigation gave the LAPD a roadmap to Jackson's below-the-waist geography, which, the accusing boy said, includes distinctive "splotches" on his buttocks and one on his penis, "which is a light color similar to the color of his face." This lurid description even pinpointed where the splotch fell while Jackson's penis was erect, the length of the performer's pubic hair, and that he was circumcised. Soon after the law enforcement's photo session with the King, he settled the Rent-a-Wreck Family's civil claim for more than $20 million.

More recently, Tom Sneddon said that the Rent-a-Wreck Family's pre-search description and drawing "corroborated" photos taken of Jackson and observations made by officers who examined the body of evidence.

While Jackson's most recent accusers have given investigators detailed accounts of Jackson's misdeeds, they are often sketchy about the timeline. The boys and their mother explain this away almost identically. Despite the outdoor giant clock often seen in aerial photography of the Neverland Ranch, the three say there were no clocks or calendars at Neverland, and they were not cognizant of the time or date. The younger boy said Jackson kept him and his brother away from "clocks and dates." The older brother told investigators that he was "not allowed" to keep track of dates and times while at the ranch.

According to testimony, it was in Miami that the King of Pop first plied the older boy with alcohol. The boy says Michael filled an empty Diet Coke can with red wine, and told the boy to "just drink it." Michael said it would relax him.

The boy said the wine gave him a headache. His younger brother told investigators that after noticing him acting weird in Miami, his older brother then confided that Michael had provided him with wine.

The young brother also told detectives that his brother would often be in the hotel suite's bathroom with Michael After being asked what they were doing, the older brother answered that they were "just talking."

The Bashir documentary aired in the US on February 6. The next day, the boy's family was flown on Michael Jackson's private plane to Neverland. With them were Michael, his two young children, a pair of nannies, and his personal physician, Dr. Alimorad Farshchian. "Jesus juice" was provided to the younger brother on that flight, which he told investigators "tasted like rubbing alcohol." Furthermore, the boy said that Michael was "acting funny" on the flight, "poking others in the butt with his foot" and passing the time by placing obscene crank calls.

Recreating Michael's behavior for investigators, the boy "physically showed us Michael's action by sticking his tongue out and moving his head, much like a cat would do when grooming," according to one investigative affidavit. When getting up to use the restroom and when everyone else onboard was asleep, the accuser's mother also saw Michael tonguing her child. She thought perhaps she was seeing things, she later told detectives. However, after talking with her younger son, she realized her eyes had not betrayed her. Also corroborating her son's testimony, the accuser's mother "mentioned seeing soda pop drinks," according to police.

In court, Bob Jones testified about Michael Jackson licking the head of one child. Jones said he while he didn't recall the incident verbatim, he admitted writing it.

> *It should too be noted that Michael Jackson has been known to kid around and perhaps this was his idea of just being silly with the boy.*
>
> *During this trial Michael has employed several lawyers, including Brian Oxman. What is interesting about Oxman is that he had always represented Michael's brothers on civil matters. Michael Jackson couldn't stand Brian Oxman. We would often see Brian on television or quoted in news articles as "Michael Jackson Attorney."*
>
> *John Branca, who has long been Michael's general counsel and represented Michael on many financial deals, would send letters to Brian Oxman requesting that he cease from calling himself Michael Jackson's attorney. Even after Michael's arrest in the current case Branca would have to send Brian letters telling him not to claim he represented Michael Jackson.*
>
> *However, because of his relationship with Randy, who began running Michael's business affairs in 2004, Oxman joined Tom Messereau as an attorney on the case. But in April 2005, in one of the more embarrassing scenes, Oxman was fired and publicly chastised in the courthouse parking lot by Messereau in full view of the mass media surrounding the lot.*

My courtroom experience was disconcerting. Just to make sure nobody could say I was paid off, I wore regular street clothes, nothing new, nothing fancy. I had nothing to hide, but I didn't want to be in Santa Maria, much less testifying against Michael Jackson. I had been with him for the better part of his life and I just couldn't help thinking about all those years. Some of them were spectacular, some were unspectacular, yet all were memorable.

Katie Jackson, the mother, Tito and Jackie greeted me kindly. They said "Hey Bob, how are you." Katie said "Hey, Bob, how are you?" It was a bit strange. These people. That family. I had known them a very long time. Worked with them, helped them, assisted them. Then I went to work for Michael and he wanted me and nobody else who worked for him to have any dealings with his family.

I walked into that courtroom and saw the fans on one side, the media on the other and the family up front. I couldn't help but look straight at Michael when I was on that witness stand. He should never have been here in the first place. I thought about the many times I had warned him about his interaction with these little boys. Perhaps he thought it was innocent behavior, but I had reminded him that not all would see it that way and that he was opening the door to unnecessary trouble.

First the prosecutor, Gordon Auchincloss questioned me. They posted e-mails I sent to Stacy Brown on the courtroom's big movie screen. Then Michael Jackson's attorney Tom Messereau questioned me, and I have to say that I was surprised at how they appeared to tread lightly with me. He didn't go after me aggressively—a surprise since Joseph's and Katherine's attorney, Debra Opri, had called me on Fox News Channel "a disgruntled ex-employee."

A lot of them assumed also that I was going to write a book detailing how Michael is a pedophile. Paranoia. Stacy Brown said it best on the witness stand. He said that Bob Jones wasn't angry with Michael Jackson, only disappointed in how the firing took place. Everybody, at some point, gets fired by Michael Jackson and it was my time. I have no problems with that. But does loyalty count for anything? It should have been handled differently. Even a lot of Michael's fans sent me e-mails expressing that sentiment.

As I left the stand in that courtroom, I wondered whether Michael too, when it was all over, would be able to walk out of there freely.

What was also a bit weird was that the District Attorney put up Stacy Brown, our attorney Mel Sachs, and me at the same hotel during our stay in the Santa Maria area. We were just five minutes from Neverland!

In fact, Stacy Brown ran into Michael and his children at their local place of worship the day before we were scheduled to testify. Stacy is one of Jehovah's Witnesses, while Michael used to be one of Jehovah's Witnesses and apparently is attempting to return to that faith.

In court papers, Detective Paul Zelis said that, after returning from Miami, the accusing family was held as "virtual prisoners." Investigators and grand jurors were told by the family that their repeated requests to leave the ranch were rejected by Michael Jackson's unindicted co-conspirators, Frank Tyson, Vincent Amen, Ronald Konitzer and Dieter Wiesner. Michael's colleagues warned that, unless they participated in the filming of a videotaped rebuttal to the BBC documentary the children would not be allowed to leave Neverland.

The accuser's mother said in court transcripts that she suspected her phone calls were monitored and she also told investigators that she was kept apart from her boys. She told police that her physical fear of Michael's manager resulted in no argument when Wiesner insisted that the family could not leave due to the supposed death threats. She quoted Konitzer as saying that if she went to the police or spoke with anyone, he would "make the kids disappear." Tyson, according to her older son, once warned him, "I could have your mother killed." He believed threats like that, he told detectives, "because Michael Jackson is a billionaire."

Shortly after the family's Neverland return, the accused mother's boyfriend, Jay Jackson, called the Santa Barbara Police Department police to report that she was being held against her will at Neverland. "I would never believe that anyone would be held prisoner at a place like Neverland," Jermaine Jackson told this author. "It's a place where you never want to leave, especially if you're a child."

The police officer who took Jay Jackson's call told him that if his girlfriend had access to a phone, she should call 911. (By the way, Jay Jackson is a forty-two-year-old Army Reserve major and no relation to Michael Jackson.)

Following up a few days later, the police were told that everything was fine, and that Jay Jackson's girlfriend (whom he has since reportedly married) was safe and back in Los Angeles.

According to some reports, over the course of the month her family stayed at Neverland, the accuser's mother frequently came and went, sometimes without her children. On February 20, she met them at the West Hills, California home of Hamid Moslehi after she agreed to have her kids videotape positive testimonials about Jackson. (Moslehi's property was also raided the same day the police hit Neverland.)

Moslehi later told the police that the accuser and his brother played video games and were relaxed while waiting for video equipment to be set up. But in police interviews, family members said that they were bullied by Michael Jackson's aides into filming the rebuttal video, which were orchestrated by Marc Schaffel, whose sidekick, Christian Robinson, conducted the video interviews.

When three DCFS representatives arrived at Jay Jackson's home on February 20, the accuser's mother "immediately went over to the VCR and started to play a video," showing her older son with Michael Jackson. A DCFS report says they then watched as Michael and the boy strolled through Neverland, rode the ranch's train, sat on a blanket, and watched the Neverland's lake's swans. During this interview, the accused mother described Jackson as "like a father" to her children and said he was "an important part of her son's recovery from cancer."

Katherine Jackson, Michael Jackson's mother, told Stacy Brown: "Why would he molest a sick child? A child he helped to get well. These people are lying." Jermaine Jackson also told Stacy Brown that his brother helped to cure the young boy by having him stay at Neverland and taken "good care of him."

In separate interviews, the three siblings also repeated the "like a father" line. However, the older grew visibly upset when social worker Karen Walker asked if he had ever been inappropriately touched. "People think that something's happened sexually between Michael and me," he said. "That's not true." The sister teared up when defending Michael as "so kind and loving." The younger boy said that trips to Neverland "make me real happy. We have fun with Michael, we all give each other nicknames. My name is Blowhole, like the fish," the boy stated in an affidavit and later testified to during the trial.

Later, the family told detectives that at that point they were too scared to tell the social workers the truth—whether about their Neverland imprisonment or Michael's inappropriate behavior. After all, they say, a Michael Jackson security guard named Asef was present when the DCSF workers arrived. However, when the interviews began, the social workers ordered Asef out. .

Notes an investigative report, "Asef warned her not to say anything wrong about Michael Jackson because they knew where her parents lived." The accused mother said Asef bugged her house with a recording device and gave her another to tape the DCFS interview. She didn't follow these instructions and tape, but she believes the woman believed Asef later retrieved the other device from the home's living room, where the DCFS interviews occurred.

The Santa Barbara Sheriff's Department conducted its own child abuse investigation. Using the DCFS interviews, Detective Terry Flaa also interviewed of the children's father David (whom their mother divorced in October 2001). The sheriff's office concluded in mid-April 2003 that the "elements of criminal activity were not met. No further action required." Soon thereafter, however, the Santa Barbara Sheriff would look at the charges and make a very different decision.

It seems the accuser's family began cooperating with law enforcement after tiring of their bullying by the Jackson camp. According to court transcripts, while the family stayed at Neverland, private eye Bradley Miller placed their scant belongings into storage.This happened after Jackson representatives found out that the accuser's mother had kept the notes Michael had sent or written her son. Later, when repeatedly trying to get their belongings back, she was rebuffed. She then hired a lawyer, but it wasn't until she began assisting the police investigation that she managed to get her stuff returned. However the notes, which had been hidden in a clay pot, were missing.

The accuser's mother told police that Jackson broke his promise to place her children in private school and to purchase them a house and an apartment (two places to move back and forth from so nobody would find them). She was also angered that Michael had given her children alcohol, especially as it posed a significant threat to her older son's very serious medical condition.

She recalled thinking that if Michael Jackson truly cared for her son, he would want him to be in America—being treated by the world's finest doctors—not hidden away in some remote Brazilian city. "She couldn't understand the urgency of them wanting the family to leave the country," one affidavit noted.

As usual, Michael Jackson had been thinking only of his own selfish needs and twisted desires. This hedonistic self-absorption and disregard for the societal norms was bound to catch up with Michael Jackson, the King of Pop, the man behind the mask.